JAMES HUDSON TAYLOR

CALLED BY GOD INTO THE
HEART OF THE DRAGON

JAMES
HUDSON
TAYLOR

CALLED BY GOD
INTO THE
HEART OF THE DRAGON

RUTH BROOMHALL

Foreword by Justin Welby, Archbishop of Canterbury

CWR

© Ruth Broomhall 2018

Published 2018 by CWR, Waverley Abbey House, Waverley Lane, Farnham, Surrey GU9 8EP, UK.

CWR is a Registered Charity – Number 294387 and a Limited Company registered in England – Registration Number 1990308.

For a list of National Distributors, visit cwr.org.uk/distributors

Scripture references are taken from the Holy Bible, New International Version® Anglicised, NIV® Copyright ©1979, 1984, 2011 by Biblica, Inc.® Used by permission. All rights reserved worldwide. Other versions used: Scripture marked ESV taken from the ESV® Bible (The Holy Bible, English Standard Version®), copyright © 2001 by Crossway, a publishing ministry of Good News Publishers. Used by permission. All rights reserved. Scripture marked AKJV taken from the Authorised King James Version. Copyright © Cambridge University Press. Used by permission. All rights reserved.

Concept development, editing, design and production by CWR.

Every effort has been made to ensure that this book contains the correct permissions and references, but if anything has been inadvertently overlooked the Publisher will be pleased to make the necessary arrangements at the first opportunity. Please contact the Publisher directly.

Cover image: OMF archives / Adobe Stock

Printed in the UK by Linney

ISBN: 978-1-78259-063-7

Dedication

This book is dedicated to the Morden family, whose recent life journeys have impacted the writing of this book. To Anne Morden, a special and valued spiritual friend, who was so interested in this book and story but who sadly passed away before it was finished. And to Peter, Rachel and Joe, may this story and this book be an encouragement and a comfort to you as you treasure the memories of a beloved wife, mother and friend.

Contents

Foreword

The story of James Hudson Taylor has been one of the most formative stories in my own Christian walk. At its heart, it is the account of a life entirely given to Christ, without reservation, for Him to use as He pleased. In that sense it mattered little whether it was as a missionary to China or, like so many of Hudson's friends, elsewhere in the world. But for Hudson it was China that had been the dream and prayer since a young age and remained his vocation and calling through his whole life, until the moment of his death near Hunan. His passion, energy and love all went to China and the Chinese. There he buried several of his children and his first wife. There he lost friends and fellow missionaries in wars, especially the Boxer rebellion. But Hudson demonstrated in word and deed that the good news of Jesus is good news for China, then as now, leading not to upheaval and instability but enabling people to form stable families, work faithfully and honestly, serve their neighbours, and care for those in need of help.

What makes Hudson so unusual? And why is it so important that his life is known today? Because although he was in one sense very much of his century, in another, he was a man out of time. So many of his attitudes, for example, to race, denomination, identity and the linking of social action with evangelistic passion, were of a later era. Or, actually of a much earlier era because they stepped out of the prejudices of the time and took on the foot-washing love of Jesus Christ. There is so much about Hudson Taylor that has inspired me since I first read a biography about him while at university: his faith, which trusted for all; his humanity, which showed in his exhaustion; his vision; his perseverance; but above all his love for Christ.

Written by a family relative, this book on Hudson Taylor includes uncompromising reflection sections at the end of each chapter, which confront us again with what it means to follow Jesus. I am glad to have read it.

Justin Welby, Archbishop of Canterbury

Introduction

'How can we magnify God who is so great? We cannot make Him greater. No; but when we use a pair of binoculars or a telescope to look, say, at the moon, we do not expect to make the moon any bigger than it is, but to bring it nearer. And when we magnify God, we do not make Him greater, but we bring Him nearer to thousands from whom He seems very far off.'[1]

It has been an honour to write the life story of James Hudson Taylor, my great-great-uncle. To be his descendant is very humbling, and the more I learn about him, the more I realise how privileged I am to share his incredible heritage. As children, my sisters and I often heard the name Hudson Taylor, and I still have books about his life that I was given as Sunday school prizes. My father, Edwin James Broomhall (Hudson Taylor's great-nephew), was a quiet man of few words (similar to his own great-grandfather, Hudson Taylor's father) while my mother (the family 'historian') read his biographies and shared fascinating anecdotes from his life with us – and still does. Her favourite words, which we all remember, were 'how he suffered!' Only now, years later, do I fully appreciate those stories and the spiritual depths they convey. Writing this book has been a very personal journey, both historically and spiritually, and it is my hope that the love, excitement and humility with which I share the story of my great-great-uncle and my own 'godly heritage' will somehow enrich this incredible story of a very ordinary man called by God into the heart of the dragon.

While Hudson Taylor's legacy rests largely in the impact of his life's work, he did leave a considerable written legacy including editing and contributing to the many volumes of *China's Millions*; a host of personal letters to family and friends, many of which were to his sister Amelia (my great-grandmother) or to his mother (my great-great-grandmother); and his own brief autobiography, *A Retrospect*. His life story, therefore, can largely

Left:
Ruth as a baby (centre) with her mother, father, sisters and her grandmother (far left), Florence (wife of Noel Broomhall)

be told through his own eyes and reflections, making this a deeply personal account of his life, character and spirituality. Alongside these, I have chosen to use three additional main texts: the two-volume history *Hudson Taylor and the China Inland Mission: Growth of a Soul* and *Growth of a Work of God* by his son Howard and daughter-in-law Geraldine (Dr and Mrs Taylor); *The Man Who Believed God* by his nephew, Marshall Broomhall; and the seven-volume history *Hudson Taylor and China's Open Century* by his great-nephew, A.J. Broomhall.

Above:
A young A.J. Broomhall

Their own familial knowledge of the man and the China Inland Mission has clearly enriched their writings, further contributing to the deeply personal nature of this account. The use of a number of secondary sources has ensured, as much as possible, both accuracy and objectivity. Where possible I have included the source of quotes; any unattributed quotes are from prior publications where the original source has not been given or from the Hudson Taylor private collection of letters.

This book is not designed to be an academic critique of either Hudson Taylor or the China Inland Mission. Rather, my aim in writing has become four-fold: to tell the life story of Hudson Taylor and the China Inland Mission; to demonstrate the power of the living God and to show, as Hudson Taylor did, the possibilities of the Christian life; to share the richness and the depth of spirituality of the man who led such an extraordinary mission; and to pass on timeless and abiding lessons that have surely become his most important legacy.

Hudson Taylor's story is extensive with so much that I would have liked to include but, unfortunately, I have had to leave out. If this book inspires you to read in greater depth and breadth, then I refer you to the books mentioned above, particularly those by Dr and Mrs Howard Taylor and A.J. Broomhall

alongside *Hudson Taylor's Legacy*, edited by Marshall Broomhall, which brings together many of Hudson Taylor's spiritual reflections in one volume.

Above: Marshall Broomhall speaking in London

I have been blessed to learn so much while researching for this book. It has been incredibly moving to read about my family history and to glean familial connections, characteristics, talents and traits! But more important than that are the spiritual depths to which this project has taken me: a journey that has been educational, inspirational, encouraging, comforting and challenging. The lessons that stand out for me include Hudson Taylor's response – personally, practically and spiritually – to adversity; his 'faith abounding'; the discipline with which he approached his life, faith and work; his love and compassion for humanity; and the depth of his love for God and commitment to a life of service. But perhaps the most challenging lesson has been how he 'held eternity in view', living his whole life – literally and spiritually – as 'a stranger in a strange land'.

Of all the words of Hudson Taylor, the following are, for me, the most moving and the most motivating:

'Love gave the blow that for a little while makes the desert more dreary but heaven more home-like. "I go to prepare a place for you": And is not our part of the preparation peopling it with those we love?'[2]

I hope and pray that all who read this book will be similarly blessed, moved, challenged and motivated by this story – the testimony of an ordinary man, fulfilling an extraordinary task, through the power and faithfulness of an almighty, loving and *living* God.

Ruth Broomhall

Above:
Ruth with her father, Edwin Broomhall

Chapter 1

A GODLY HERITAGE

(1776–1832)

'But as for me and my household,
we will serve the LORD.'
(Joshua 24:15)

E ven before he was born, God's hand was shaping and moulding the life of James Hudson Taylor. His newly-married parents, James and Amelia Taylor, were keen to devote their lives to Christ and the gospel. One day, moved by a particular passage in the Bible, James Taylor sat down with his wife to share the reading with her. As they meditated on the words in front of them, they realised that God was speaking directly to them. They were in the presence of God, with the clear command: 'Consecrate to me your firstborn'. The moment is best captured by Howard and Geraldine Taylor, son and daughter-in-law of Hudson Taylor, in their biography, *Hudson Taylor in Early Years – The Growth of a Soul*:

'But it was to God above all James Taylor sought to be faithful, and he was possessed by a profound conviction of His infinite faithfulness. He took the Bible very simply, believing it was of all books the most practical if put to the test of experience. In this too he met with fullest sympathy from the young wife who was herself so loyal to the Lord.

'On a day they could never forget, in their first winter together, he sought her Bible in hand to talk over a passage that had impressed him. It was part of the thirteenth chapter of Exodus, with the corresponding verses in Numbers: "Sanctify unto me all the firstborn... All the firstborn are mine... Mine shall they be... Set apart unto the Lord."

'Long and earnest was the talk that followed in view of the happiness to which they were looking forward. Their hearts held back nothing from the Lord. With them it was not a question of how little could be given, but how much. Did the Lord claim the best gift of His own giving? Their child was more their own for being His. To such parents what could be more welcome than the invitation, nay command, to set apart their dearest thus to him? And how precious the Divine assurance, "It is Mine", not for time only but for eternity.

'Together they knelt in the silence to fulfil as literally as *possible an obligation they could not relegate to Hebrew parents of old. It was no ceremony to be gone through merely but a definite transaction, the handing over of their best to God, recalling which the mother wrote long after: "This act of consecration they solemnly performed upon their knees, asking for the rich influence of the Holy Spirit, that their firstborn might be 'set apart' indeed from that hour."*

'And just as definitely the Lord responded, giving them faith to realise that he had accepted the gift; that henceforth the life so dear to them was their own no longer, but must be held at the disposal of a higher claim, a deeper love than theirs."

Amelia was already carrying their first child. In the spring of the following year, on 21 May 1832, their firstborn son, the child they had consecrated to God in prayer, was born. His name, James Hudson Taylor, forever joined together as one the godly heritage of his parents – 'the influence of whose lives will never pass away'. It is a name and a heritage that lives on. James Hudson Taylor's extraordinary life story is a timeless example of the possibilities of a life possessed with an unshakeable belief in the living God.

James Hudson Taylor was born into a godly home and heritage, his spiritually-rich ancestry clearly part of God's amazing plan for his life. The starting point for this 'godly heritage' can be traced back to Hudson Taylor's great-grandparents, James and Elizabeth (Betty) Taylor, and the Methodist revival of the eighteenth century. The great conversion stories of James and Betty Taylor were to prove vital in the preparation for Hudson Taylor's future calling. Their stories also demonstrate two faith principles already at work in the Taylor family that were to become foundational to the future work and mission of the man called by God to China – the faithfulness of God and the power of prayer.

Right:
James Hudson Taylor and some of his descendants

至於我，和我家
我們必定事奉耶和華

BUT AS FOR ME AND MY
HOUSE, WE WILL SERVE THE LORD.

JAMES HUDSON TAYLOR
*1854-1905

HERBERT HUDSON TAYLOR
*1881-1932

戴永晃
JAMES HUDSON TAYLOR II
*1917-1967

戴繼宗
JAMES HUDSON TAYLOR IV

戴紹曾
JAMES HUDSON TAYLOR III
*1955-

*在中國宣教的年代
years of missionary service in China

Great-grandparents: James and Betty Taylor

John Wesley, a leading Methodist figure and itinerant preacher, had visited Mapplewell, Yorkshire (now Staincross), the home town of James Taylor, preaching to crowds in the local market place. James had shown no interest in the message brought by John Wesley; however, his neighbours, Joseph and 'Dame Betty' Shaw, had, and soon their house became a hub of hospitality for visiting preachers. Even here we see God's providence in situating James Taylor in the house next door. James may have chosen to ignore the message brought by these travelling preachers, but he could not avoid witnessing the impact of it on those around him.

On the day of James Taylor's wedding, 1 February 1776, his bride and local girl, Betty Johnson, was waiting for him at the Anglican church in Royston, Yorkshire. Before that day, neither of them had given much thought to anything to do with God – but God had other plans. As James was carrying sheaves of wheat from the field to the barn on that frosty wedding day morning, he could hear hymns being sung from the cottage next door. Perhaps it was this that turned his thoughts to God and to the words: 'as for me and my household, we will serve the LORD' (Joshua 24:15). These words refused to leave the young bridegroom, and soon he was on his knees, giving his life – and that of his future family or 'house' – to his Saviour.

The church bells were ringing as James Taylor ran the two miles to Royston to meet his bride, and after a short service James and Betty were declared man and wife. As they left the church together, James explained to Betty what had taken place earlier that day. His new bride was dismayed. The music, dancing and revelry that she had expected to be a part of their married life would now be replaced with Bible reading, prayers and hymn singing. It is fair to say that the first days of married life were not happy ones! While James remained utterly faithful in his commitment to his newly discovered Lord and Saviour, Betty was determined to make his life as uncomfortable as she could with her grumblings, reproaches and refusal to join in family worship and prayers.

James put up with this as long as he could. But then one day, his patience wearing thin, he picked Betty up in his arms, carried her upstairs and, kneeling beside her, proceeded to pour out his

heart to God in prayer for his wife. The impact on Betty was great. Although she didn't show it at first, her heart had been moved. A deep sense of her own sin in relation to God had begun to take hold of her and she found herself wishing for the same peace that she saw in her husband. The next evening, when James brought out the Bible for family worship as usual, Betty was happy to listen. God was moving in her life too and, as her husband prayed, Betty gave her life to Christ. The two were now united in faith as well as in marriage. God's faithfulness towards James and the power of prayer had both been evident in their individual conversion experiences, and so began the blessings of God on the Taylor family that were to continue for many years to come.

A few years after their marriage, James and Betty moved to the nearby town of Barnsley in Yorkshire, where James became a local preacher and class leader[2] of the Methodist Society. Their simple home became the first Methodist 'Church in the House', with Betty's kitchen a focal point. Then, in 1786, James and Betty had the privilege of hosting John Wesley on one of his visits to Barnsley. This visit, by one of the founding fathers of the Methodist revival, was to prove the first of many wonderfully providential connections between the Taylor family line and other great men and women of faith.[3]

Sadly, James did not enjoy good health and died in 1795 leaving a widow and several children. But despite his early death, his legacy was still a significant one. He was instrumental in the building and opening of the first Wesleyan chapel in Barnsley. But perhaps most significantly to this story, he and Betty had passed down to their children, and their children's children, the richest of all inheritances – a godly home, tradition, and Christian role models. Their eldest son John, only 17 years of age when his father died, was already in employment and a hard worker, and so was able to take his father's place in supporting the family. Then, at the age of just 21, John married Mary Shepherd, the daughter of William Shepherd, a contemporary of John Wesley. Mary inherited from her father 'unusual strength of mind and body, as well as principles of sincere and simple godliness'.[4] So we witness the same 'godly heritage' that John had grown up with continuing in his married life with Mary. Together they would become the grandparents of James Hudson Taylor.

Grandparents: John and Mary Taylor

John and Mary Taylor made their first home on Pinfold Hill, near the Wesleyan chapel. It was by all accounts a happy home. John and Mary were both class leaders at the chapel, and John was noted particularly for his strong vocal and musical abilities. Church life thrived. Following the example of Robert Raikes who was a pioneer of the Sunday school movement, John Whitworth (a

Above: John Taylor's home in Barnsley

local architect) started up a Sunday school, and on the opening day had over 600 children crowding in! By 1810, a school building to house the Sunday school had been erected and a larger chapel built. John Wesley's words 'surely God will have a people in this place'[5], recorded in his diary on Friday, 30 June 1786 when he visited Barnsley and stayed with James and Betty Taylor, were 'surely' proving true.

John's business as a reed-maker also prospered, giving him the means to have built a more substantial stone house in Barnsley, situated on the corner of Pitt Street and York Street. Family life was busy, with seven children surviving to reach adulthood. The four sons all enjoyed a sound education and were allowed to choose their own way in life: John, the eldest, took up his father's business, William became a stockbroker in Manchester, and Samuel became a Wesleyan minister. James, the father of Hudson Taylor, had wanted to study medicine but circumstances did not permit this, so he settled for chemistry as the next best thing. An apprenticeship took him away from home to a neighbouring town for seven years, and by the age of 21 he had grown into a mature and sensible young man.

Parents: James and Amelia Taylor

Above:
James and
Amelia Taylor

Hudson Taylor's father was 'an omnivorous reader', particularly of theology. He loved to read the Bible, sermons and biographies. He had some aptitude for music and mathematics, and was devoted to the study of birds, plants and nature generally – a passion that Hudson Taylor himself shared throughout his own life. James Taylor was not a tall man, but he was 'strong and active, and with a bright smile and pleasant manner... decidedly prepossessing'.[6] At the age of 19 he was accepted as an accredited preacher for the

Wesleyan Methodist Church, and within five years commenced his own business as a chemist at 21 Cheapside, right in the heart of Barnsley, thanks to a loan advanced to him by his father.

For several years James had harboured strong affections for 'the girl next door'. In 1824, Amelia Hudson had moved into the church manse situated on the opposite side of the street to the Taylor's house. She was the daughter of Rev Benjamin Hudson, the minister of the Wesleyan chapel and a talented artist with a great sense of humour, well-loved and respected by the local community. His wife is described as having 'a strength and sweetness of spirit'.[7] They had seven children (three boys and four girls), three of whom became talented portrait painters. Amelia was gifted with a beautiful singing voice, inspiring James Taylor to affectionately call her 'the nightingale'.

Romance blossomed between James and Amelia and they became engaged when they were both still teenagers. Life commitments and necessities, however, meant they had to spend some years apart: James as a young apprentice in Rotherham, and Amelia as a governess to three children in Castle Donnington. It wasn't until 5 April 1831 that James and Amelia were finally married at St Mary's Church in Barton-on-Humber (where Amelia's father was now the minister) and the names Hudson and Taylor were united. James was now 24 years old and well-established with a thriving, debt-free business; Amelia was a year younger. As a happily married couple, these sweethearts made their home in Barnsley and their spiritual life together grew. James became a Methodist class leader and a local lay preacher, and Amelia actively supported him. History records a revival at Barnsley Chapel and many young people became followers of Christ.

James and Amelia were blessed with five children: James

Above:
Benjamin
Hudson

Hudson (the subject of this book), William Shepherd, Amelia Hudson who later married Benjamin Broomhall,[8] Theodore and Louisa Shepherd (preserving the Shepherd family name). Both William and Theodore died young, leaving James Hudson with the companionship of his two sisters. Amelia was closer in age to James, and so it was perhaps natural that a close bond developed between them, which, as teenagers, became routed in a shared faith and spirituality. This remained strong and unbroken to the end, even though for much of their adult lives they were separated by vast distances and varying cultures.

James and Amelia Taylor were devoted parents, delighting in their children and in their God. We are told that they were 'worthy complements' to one another, so that what their father lacked, their mother supplied, and vice versa. James Taylor was a powerful man and quite forceful, whereas Amelia's government of the home was 'more by love than law'.[9] It was a secure home and a disciplined upbringing that Hudson Taylor, in later life, was to look back on with love and respect, a foundation utterly necessary for the extraordinary task to which God would call him.

'For myself, and the work I have been permitted to do for God, I owe an unspeakable debt of gratitude to my beloved and honoured parents who have entered into rest, but the influence of whose lives will never pass away.'[10]

God's chosen school

What was it about the family life of James and Amelia that made it so foundational to the future work of their son James Hudson Taylor? We have already considered the spiritual heritage that began with the conversions of James and Betty Taylor and then passed down to succeeding generations. To this rich spiritual heritage, James and Amelia added their own particular characters and gifts. James had a strength of character and a great intellect, combined with a strong sense of duty and a perfectionist nature that could be hard to live up to. As already mentioned, he was a stern disciplinarian but also a highly respected and trusted member of the community, and if he was strict with others, he was no less strict with himself. His grandson, Marshall Broomhall, describes him thus:

> 'His deep sense of responsibility to God, his upright dealings with men, his scrupulous care to be honourable in all things, and his unquestioned integrity, soon commanded the esteem and confidence of his fellowmen. And behind and beneath that powerful exterior beat a large and kindly heart, for he was full of good works and gracious deeds, especially to any who were in need or sorrow.'[11]

James Taylor was 'a man possessed of a strong, personal faith in God as the living God, and in His unchanging faithfulness'. It was a faith that James Taylor was careful to model to his children, and that Hudson Taylor, his son, came to rest on as he fulfilled his calling. Prayer and daily devotions were not just habits instilled in the children from an early age: their father ensured that 'a sense of the reality and presence of God was communicated to his children'. So while family prayers were a sacred institution, a definite time was also set aside for the children's own private devotions. In this way James encouraged them to have a relationship with the living God. Marshall Broomhall sums up well the vitality of James' spiritual fatherliness for the young Hudson Taylor: 'All this early training in childlike faith in God, and in God's promises, was of inestimable value to Hudson Taylor in years to come. Foundations were then laid in things of the Spirit without which many of the constructive enterprises of the future would have been impossible.'

Alongside a strong and disciplined spiritual training, James Taylor passed down a thoroughness in business practice. Attention to detail was displayed in all transactions and debts were paid immediately. His scrupulous nature, combined with exactitude in the realm of mathematics, led the people of the town to appoint him as manager to the Barnsley Permanent Building Society in 1853. James Taylor's precision and ability with money and other matters was to prove another vital training ground for his young son. This was surely 'God's chosen school' for the boy who was to become founder and leader of the China Inland Mission.

Hudson Taylor's mother Amelia was no less influential, as Marshall Broomhall recounts:

> *'But the mother of the home was cast in a gentler mould, yet without any touch of weakness. While always supporting the father's authority she knew how to comfort and to soothe... Her very presence brought a sense of calm and tranquillity, and to her quiet, loving, tactful ways young Hudson and his sisters owed no less than to their father. If he supplied the driving force of life, she poured in the oil. She was an excellent housewife too, and with the aid of one maid made her home a model of smooth running. Slovenliness was never allowed, while diligence, neatness, and order were unfailingly required, until they became the habits of the children.'*

It was Amelia who was responsible in the main for her children's education, and she proved an excellent teacher. We read that she excelled in English and was exacting in her expectation regarding language, grammar, enunciation and pronunciation. Such close attention to words and sounds must have been of inestimable value to Hudson Taylor as he prepared for mission in China: a working knowledge of the Chinese language demands accuracy in both tone and emphasis. Once again, we see God's amazing planning at work in the life of the young Hudson Taylor.

As we follow the life of James Hudson Taylor, it will become increasingly clear just how foundational his 'godly heritage' was. One generation impacts another, but it is our parents that are surely the greatest influence on our formation. This is most certainly seen in the joint contribution of Hudson Taylor's father and mother from whom Hudson 'inherited that strength of character; that resolute determination to do his duty; that unshaken faith in God, which carried him through many a seemingly impossible task; that love and consideration for others; and that gentle humble spirit, which in honour preferred others to himself. What made him so approachable were those gentle qualities inherited from his mother; yet beneath all these, though not always seen by men, were those powerful reserves of strength and resolution, and that almost lion-like determination, bequeathed him by his father.' His was indeed a rich, vital, and precise heritage.

Reflection – The faithfulness of God

'If we believe not, yet he abideth faithful: he cannot deny himself' *(2 Timothy 2:13, AKJV)*

Hudson Taylor was a man who believed in a living, powerful, all-faithful God. Throughout his life he exercised incredible faith, following Christ across the oceans to China and laying his entire life – and the lives of his family – on the altar for God's service. The story of Hudson Taylor's life, from his 'godly heritage', the consecration of his life by his parents before he was even born, through to the fulfilment of his calling, is saturated with examples of this absolute and unswerving faith in the faithfulness of God.

> *'"The legacy which Bunyan has left us," writes Dr Fullerton, "is the assurance of grace. Grace! Grace abounding! Grace abounding to the chief of sinners! Not only is this the*

overwhelming subject of his great book, it is the one line upon which all his experience is threaded and the one theme to which he inevitably returns, no matter where he begins. In spite of the wonderful variety of his writings he is almost like Paganini playing on one string."

'With the alteration of one word only this passage might have been written of Hudson Taylor. Substitute "faith" for "grace" and not another change is necessary. The legacy Hudson Taylor has left us is the assurance of faith. Faith! Faith in God! Hold the faithfulness of God! Though we deny Him, yet He abideth faithful. This was the dominant message of his life, like the recurrent theme of a fugue. Though his contribution to the Christian church is rich and varied, this is its outstanding feature. Faith in God was the strength of his life, and the explanation of his achievements.'[12]

Hudson Taylor's faith was an audacious one. It was a faith that believed in the impossible and responded accordingly. His faith in the faithfulness of God enabled him to lead a mission that exercised, throughout his lifetime, a 'pure faith' policy. Missionaries were required to 'obey and go'. Members of the mission prayed in faith and did not make specific needs known. Collection boxes were not allowed at public meetings. Instead, Hudson Taylor simply pleaded the cause for Christ in China, living close to God and seeking *His* will in every step he took. The work of the China Inland Mission was God's work, done in God's way, so God would provide.

Such was Hudson Taylor's faith in the faithfulness of God. It was not Hudson Taylor's great faith that was the key to the success of the China Inland Mission; it was his faith in a *great and faithful God.*

認為 Think

When we think of the word 'faithful' we often think of it in relation to our (both individual and universal) faithfulness to God. But an important message we learn through the story of Hudson Taylor, starting with his father and forefathers, is that real power comes with a recognition of God's faithfulness to us. In Hudson Taylor's own words: 'There are two sides of faith. There is the God-ward side, and there is the man-ward side. It is when God's faithfulness is fully recognised by us that we shall be enabled to rest in quiet confidence and faith that He will fulfil His word.'[13]

Hudson Taylor was taught to recognise God's faithfulness from an early age, and came to rest on it. His unwavering belief in the faithfulness of God enabled him to trust God even in incredibly challenging circumstances. He learnt that God could be trusted even when man failed: 'If we believe not, yet he abideth faithful: he cannot deny himself' (2 Timothy 2:13, AKJV).

響應 Respond

Hudson Taylor's background leaves us much to ponder in relation to our own lives and legacy. No family is perfect and doubtless there were many imperfections in the lives of Hudson Taylor's ancestors, but these must surely fade into insignificance when we consider the lasting impact of the lives of these godly men and women on their children and children's children. Hudson Taylor was blessed in being surrounded by 'every influence and definite instruction that could impress him with the sense of God and with the importance of godly living' from the moment he was born.[14]

Have you been inspired to encourage your children, grandchildren, godchildren or extended families to develop a relationship with a living, all-powerful and *faithful* God? How can you ensure this becomes a priority?

> 'Hold God's faithfulness – have faith in God.'

Chapter 2

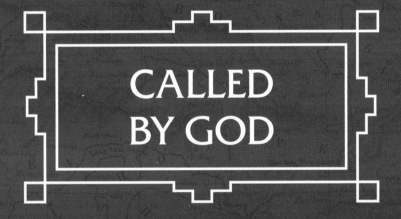

CALLED
BY GOD

(1832–1849)

*'When I am a man, I will be
a missionary, and go to China.'*[1]

As a child, Hudson Taylor was considered too delicate to attend school so, save for a brief interlude at around the age of eleven, he received all his education at home. The majority of this was delivered by his mother, Amelia; however his father, James Taylor, being an avid reader with a strong intellect, also took an interest and supervised some subjects. Both father and son were blessed with an aptitude for languages: James Taylor commenced the study of Chinese at the age of 70, and Hudson Taylor would advocate to new missionaries that a working knowledge of the Chinese language could be acquired in just six months. Incredibly, thanks to the instruction of his father, Hudson Taylor had learned the Hebrew alphabet before he was four years old!

Evidence suggests that the young Hudson benefitted hugely from this structured but varied education. Not only was he encouraged to develop language skills that were to prove of lasting value to his future calling, he came to share in his father's love of nature – both flora and fauna – a hobby that was to help sustain him through some of the most challenging circumstances on the mission field. Perhaps the most providential of all his early schooling was his father's interest in China and passion for people to know God, a passion which inspired Hudson Taylor to say, when still just a small child, 'when I am a man, I will be a missionary, and go to China'.

James Taylor had himself longed to go to China, but it had not been possible. Despite this, his interest in China continued, spurred by a desire to see the gospel proclaimed in that vast and spiritually needy land. He often prayed that, if God blessed him with a son, his son might go to China instead of him. Interestingly, Hudson Taylor was not told of these prayers until seven years after he had sailed to China for the first time, possibly because his delicate constitution had convinced his parents that he would never be strong enough to go. But as a young child, Hudson was given many opportunities to learn about the country for which his father cared so intensely, including reading about China in the many books found in his father's library. Reading aloud and privately were both actively encouraged in the Taylor home. In this way, Hudson and his siblings 'had their hearts and minds enlarged by many a book of travel and history'. Among the many books on China, the young Hudson and Amelia became very interested in a book called *Peter Parley's Tales about China and the Chinese*, a book 'they read again and again, until the sister, too, resolved to accompany her brother to that strange and distant country'. [2]

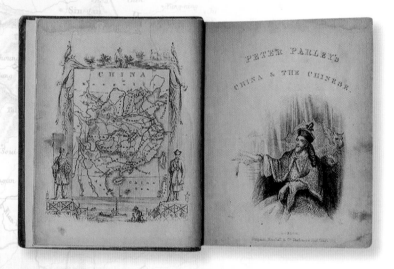

Right:
Early edition of Peter Parley's book on China

Then there were the meetings and social occasions that his parents frequently held in the drawing room over their chemist premises in 21 Cheapside, Barnsley. Conversation would be lively and varied, with topics including politics, theology, sermons, and mission work at home and abroad. Considering James Taylor's abiding interest in China, it is almost certain that that large, nonbelieving land featured heavily in these conversations. The children were present during these occasions and so, understandably, lasting memories and influences were formed in their young hearts and minds.

In 1839, when Hudson was just a young lad of seven, the Methodists celebrated their centenary year. Marshall Broomhall records that some of Hudson Taylor's 'first definite spiritual experiences in his life'[3] were connected with these centenary celebrations. Special Methodist meetings were held around Yorkshire, and Hudson would often accompany his father to them, taking great delight when people become followers of Christ. His response was surely a sign that God was already at work in the heart of the young Hudson Taylor, while the very nature of these meetings would have given him a taste of what John Bunyan called 'awakening and converting work'[4] – work that was to become his life's passion and purpose.

Methodists also sought to celebrate the centenary with new missionary endeavours to various parts of the world. Sadly, for missionaries at that time, China was 'a closed land'. In the *Protestant Missionary Atlas of the World*, published in London in 1839, China is not even marked on the map. This caused James Taylor much concern. 'Why do we not send missionaries there?' he would frequently exclaim. One wonders just how much these words influenced the heart of his young son, who would one day be 'called by God' to take the gospel to that vast and forgotten land.

'The finished work of Christ'

But before Hudson Taylor could be called by God to China, he needed to accept God's call to follow Him and become a Christian. Clearly God was at work in the life of the young Hudson, his 'godly heritage' training him in the ways of God from a very early age. And Hudson responded, with both heart and mind. In 1846, at the age of 14, Hudson Taylor made 'his first definite surrender of himself to God'[5] after reading a leaflet published by the Religious Tract Society. 'From my earliest childhood I have felt the strivings of the Holy Spirit, and... about fourteen years of age I gave my heart to God', wrote Hudson Taylor some few years later. It was an experience born, as he himself recognised, from a spiritual journey that had commenced many years earlier. It was not to be until a few years later, though, that Hudson Taylor came to fully rest on Christ as his own personal Lord and Saviour. God had planned a particular journey to the cross for the young Hudson, a journey that included a brief time of scepticism and worldly influences.

At 15 years old, Hudson Taylor obtained a post in a Barnsley bank and went to work – albeit briefly due to some temporary eye trouble – among men who had their sights fixed on more worldly pleasures and influences. Still a young lad and impressionable, Hudson found himself drawn to them and their ideas. Wealth was not the only attraction; the scepticism towards God and Christians shown by his colleagues began to eat away at him, until he found himself questioning his own faith. In later years, Hudson Taylor reflected on this time as part of God's providential planning. Not only was the brief experience in banking of huge benefit in his future role as founder and leader of the China Inland Mission (CIM), but he also found this period of scepticism to be of great value. In Hudson Taylor's own words:

'It may seem strange to say it, but I have often felt thankful for the experience of this time of scepticism. The inconsistencies of Christian people, who while professing to believe their Bibles were yet content to live just as they would if there were no such book, had been one of the strongest arguments of my sceptical companions; and I frequently felt at that time, and said, that if I pretended to believe the Bible I would at any rate attempt to live by it, putting it fairly to the test, and if it failed to prove true and reliable, would throw it overboard altogether. These views I retained when the Lord was pleased to bring me to Himself; and I think I may say that since then I have put God's word to the test. Certainly it has never failed me. I have never had reason to regret the confidence I have placed in its promises, or to deplore following the guidance I have found in its directions.'[6]

Although the exact cause of his vision problems is not known, Hudson Taylor's poor eyesight meant that he was forced to leave the bank and influences that could so easily have taken his attention away from God. He called this God's 'infinite mercy' – a reflection of his lifelong attitude to suffering, which would enable him, in all his missionary endeavours, to find strength and peace in even the most terrible and tragic of circumstances. God was most certainly preparing the way for Hudson Taylor. Interestingly, although there are some images of Hudson Taylor wearing glasses as a young man, there is no mention of any continuing sight problem, and we only see him wearing glasses again in his later years.

The time of Hudson Taylor's renewed desire to follow Christ is recorded in detail in his autobiography entitled *A Retrospect*, written much later in 1894. This significant moment also gives us a flavour of the shared spirituality within the Taylor family:

'Let me tell you how God answered the prayers of my dear mother and of my beloved sister, now Mrs Broomhall, for my conversion. On a day which I shall never forget, when I was about fifteen years of age,[7] my dear mother being absent from home, I had a holiday, and in the afternoon looked through my father's library to find some book with which to while away the unoccupied hours. Nothing attracting me, I turned over a little basket of pamphlets, and selected from amongst them a Gospel tract which looked interesting, saying to myself, "there will be a story at the commencement, and a sermon or moral at the close: I will take the former and leave the latter for those who like it."

'I sat down to read the little book in an utterly unconcerned state of mind, believing indeed at the time that if there were any salvation it was not for me, and with a distinct intention to put away the tract as soon as it should seem prosy... Little did I know at the time what was going on in the heart of my dear mother, seventy or eighty miles away. She rose from the dinner table that afternoon with an intense yearning for the conversion of her boy, and feeling that – absent from home, *and having more leisure than she could otherwise secure – a special opportunity was afforded her of pleading with God on my behalf. She went to her room and turned the key in the door, resolved not to leave that spot until her prayers were answered. Hour after hour did that dear mother plead for me, until at length she could pray no longer, but was constrained to praise God for that which His Spirit taught her had already been accomplished – the conversion of her only son.*

Right:
Pages from *Poor Richard* tract

The text of the tract pages reads:

POOR RICHARD.

On the following day, an aged servant of God, (Mr. G.) being taken to see Poor Richard, happened to ask him how old he was. Richard thought he referred to his spiritual birth, and answered, "I am only four days old, Sir." He then spoke of the last Lord's day evening, when he had found peace; and turning to the sister through whom the Lord had been pleased thus to bless his soul, he said "We shall talk of that evening, and praise God for it, when we are in heaven together."

During a subsequent visit he spoke of his neighbours—how his heart yearned over them—how he wished they might every one come to Jesus as he had; and said how happy it made him to think that the Lord's children were going about telling sinners about Jesus, whom he felt to be so precious to him. He was asked if he liked to see the Lord's children himself. His answer was, "My heart bounds with joy when they come in, as they come to speak about Jesus."

Two days before he died, he was visited by Mr. D——, a Christian who labours much for the Lord in preaching the Gospel. He was in perfect peace, and Mr. D—— read to him Rev. vii., from verse 9 to the end, and said, "You will see Jesus before I shall, Richard. I should like to be with Jesus." Richard replied that he hoped Mr. D—— might have a little longer, as he was able to tell of the love of Jesus to poor sinners. Mr. D—— then said to him, "Richard, what will you sing when you get there. Will you sing of your own goodness?" He answered, "I'll sing of nothing but the precious blood of the Lamb."

In the course of the night of Friday, 4th of July, (the night before he died) he said to his wife, "Oh! how I love you!" She asked him if he troubled at leaving her and his children. He said,

"No; for I trust, the same Jesus that had mercy on me, will have mercy on you, and will care for them." As long as he was able to speak that night, he continued saying, "Precious Jesus!"

On the next morning (Saturday), a little before four o'clock, two poor brethren in the Lord, on their way to their daily labour, went in to see if Poor Richard was yet alive, and saw him for the last time on earth. Consciousness was gone; he lay quite still and calm, and apparently happy. They remained a little while by his bed-side, and prayed over him, that the Lord Jesus would be with him in the valley of the shadow of death, and that he might depart in peace. Their prayer was heard, and at half-past six o'clock that same morning he quietly fell asleep in Jesus.

In closing this little narrative of dear Richard E——, I would only desire to call the attention of the reader to one marked feature in his conversion; and that is, his unbroken joy and peace directly he was enabled to rest on the word of God respecting Jesus. He believed God's testimony about the work of Christ, and he was satisfied. He did not look into his own heart to find out *there* whether Christ had died for him; but he trusted in the word of God about it. The same word that told him he was a sinner, told him that Christ died for the chief of sinners, and that was all he wanted to know. It was enough. God had himself provided the Lamb. God had himself caused the Lamb to be slain. God had declared that the blood of the Lamb was sufficient; and therefore, why might not Poor Richard trust in its full and eternal value? He knew himself unworthy; but God said, Christ was precious. He knew his own heart was hard and evil; but it was Christ who had died; and His death alone saves sinners, and not the state of

'I, in the meantime, had been led in the way I have mentioned to take up this little tract, and while reading it was struck with the sentence, "The finished work of Christ." The thought passed through my mind, "Why does the author use this expression? Why not say the atoning or propitiatory work of Christ?" Immediately the words "It is finished" suggested themselves to my mind. What was finished? And I at once replied, "A full and perfect atonement and satisfaction for sin: the debt was paid by the Substitute; Christ died for our sins, and not for ours only, but also for the sins of the whole world." Then came the thought, "If the whole work was finished and the whole debt paid, what is there left for me to do?" And with this dawned the joyful

Left:
Amelia Taylor

conviction, as light was flashed into my soul by the Holy Spirit, that there was nothing in the world to be done but to fall down on one's knees, and accepting this Saviour and His salvation, to praise Him forevermore. Thus while my dear mother was praising God on her knees in her chamber, I was praising Him in the old warehouse to which I had gone alone to read at my leisure this little book.

'Several days elapsed 'ere I ventured to make my beloved sister the confidante of my joy, and then only after she had promised not to tell anyone of my soul secret. When our dear mother came home a fortnight later, I was the first to meet her at the door, and to tell her I had such glad news to give. I can almost feel that dear mother's arms around my neck, as she pressed me to her bosom and said, "I know, my boy; I have been rejoicing for a fortnight in the glad tidings you have to tell me." "Why," I asked in surprise, "has Amelia broken her promise? She said she would tell no one." My dear mother assured me that it was not from any human source that she had learned the tidings, and went on to tell the little incident motioned above. You will agree with me that it would be strange indeed if I were not a believer in the power of prayer.

'Nor was this all. Some little time after, I picked up a pocket book exactly like one of my own, and thinking that it was mine, opened it. The lines that caught my eye were an entry in the little diary, which belonged to my sister, to the effect that she would give herself daily to prayer until God should answer in the conversion of her brother. Exactly one month later the Lord was pleased to turn me from darkness to light.

'Brought up in such a circle and saved under such circumstances it was perhaps natural that from the commencement of my Christian life, I was led to feel that the promises were very real, and that prayer was in sober matter of fact transacting business with God, whether on one's own behalf or on behalf of those for whom one sought His blessing.'[8]

It was not to be long before Hudson Taylor was again 'transacting business with God', this time about the very land and people that he had heard so much about as a child – China and the Chinese people who had not heard about God's love.

Called to China: A 'covenant with the Almighty'

Hudson Taylor's call to China was no less dramatic, no less definite than his conversion: a call that became clearer over a number of stages, the first stage occurring just a few weeks following his conversion. Full of joy over what had happened, Hudson longed to give his life in service to his Lord. So, one afternoon, in the summer of 1849, Hudson retired to his room to pray. Later he recounted:

'Well do I remember that occasion, how in the gladness of my heart I poured out my soul before God; and again and again confessing my grateful love to Him who had done everything for me – who had saved me when I had given up all hope and even desire for salvation – I besought Him to give me some work to do for Him, as an outlet for love and gratitude; some self-denying service, no matter what it might be, however trying or trivial; something with which He would be pleased, and that I might do for Him who had done so much for me. Well do I remember, as in unreserved consecration I put myself, my life, my friends, my all, upon the altar, the deep solemnity that came over my soul with the assurance that my offering was accepted. The presence of God became unutterably

real and blessed; and though but a child under sixteen, I remember stretching myself on the ground, and lying there silent before Him with unspeakable awe and unspeakable joy. For what service I knew not; but a deep consciousness that I was no longer my own took possession of me, which has never since been effaced. It has been a very practical consciousness.'[9]

The specific call to China did not follow immediately. Instead, Hudson experienced a few months of 'painful deadness of soul, with much conflict',[10] particularly difficult coming so soon after his conversion. Finally, on 2 December 1849, he poured out his soul in a letter to his sister Amelia, desperately pleading with her to pray for him. When the letter was finished and the envelope sealed, Hudson Taylor tried to sleep, but sleep eluded him, so he took to prayer. Howard and Geraldine Taylor continue the story:

'And then, alone upon his knees, a great purpose arose within him. If only God would work on his behalf, would break the power of sin and save him, spirit, soul and body, for time and for eternity, he would renounce all earthly prospects and be utterly at His disposal. He would go anywhere, do anything, suffer whatever His cause might demand, and be wholly given to His will and service. This was the cry of his heart; nothing held back – if only God would deliver him and keep him from falling.'

Instinctively we pause and turn aside from a scene so sacred. The place is holy ground. Of what transpired further we know no more, save for a few lines written when occasion required it the following year. For he rarely referred to this experience, though all life lived it out.

'"Never shall I forget," he wrote, "the feeling that came over me then. Words can never describe it. I felt I was in the presence of God, entering into covenant with the Almighty.

I felt as though I wished to withdraw my promise, but could not. Something seemed to say, 'Your prayer is answered, your conditions are accepted.' And from that time the conviction never left me that I was called to China.'"[11]

Hudson Taylor arose from his knees, full of joy for what had taken place. Immediately, he went to the envelope which, moments before, he had sealed in readiness for posting. It was not too late to tell his sister that the prayers for which he had asked her had, in fact, already been answered. The brief postscript Hudson added to the letter reveals the 'abundant joy' that was, at last, his:

'Bless the Lord, O my soul, and all that is within me shout His praise! Glory to God, my dear Amelia. Christ has said: "Seek, and ye shall find", and praise His Name, He has revealed Himself to me in an overflowing manner. He has cleansed me from all sin, from all my idols. He has given me a new heart. Glory, glory, glory, to His ever-blessed Name! I cannot write for joy. I open my letter to tell you.'[12]

Hudson Taylor's mother later wrote about this moment. It was, she recalled, as if God himself had spoken. The command was given: 'Then go for me to China' and the command was obeyed.[13] From that moment on Hudson Taylor's life, work and mission was resolutely focused on China.

Reflection – The power of prayer

'Do not be anxious about anything, but in every situation, by prayer and petition, with thanksgiving, present your requests to God.' *(Philippians 4:6)*

The story of Hudson Taylor and the CIM demonstrates very clearly the power of prayer. In the account of his conversion, the prayers of three people were answered: those of his mother and his sister, both of whom were praying for the conversion of Hudson; and Hudson's own prayers of repentance and praise. Peace came over Hudson Taylor's mother as she prayed, 'joyful conviction' came over Hudson Taylor as the Holy Spirit opened his eyes to 'the finished work of Christ', and the family shared in joy and praise for God with the realisation that their prayers had been answered. So there was power in their prayers, but there was also purpose. Prayers answered deepen our faith and spur us on to pray more.

Hudson Taylor had witnessed the absolute and unequivocal power of prayer early on in his Christian life. It was an experience he was never to forget. From that moment on Hudson Taylor was a passionate believer in the power, the purpose and the practice of prayer. Prayer became a foundational principle and practice for Hudson Taylor personally and for the CIM. Strong, intentional, believing prayer, both privately and as a group, was of absolute importance. Hudson Taylor once claimed that the sun never rose on China without finding him at prayer. Prayer was his primary business. 'You can work without praying', stated Hudson Taylor, 'but it is a bad plan. But you cannot pray in earnest without working. Do not be so busy with work for Christ that you have no strength left for praying. True prayer requires strength.'[14]

It was also the primary business of the CIM. There was a regular practice of prayer and fasting before all decision making, and New Year's Eve was set aside every year as the CIM's annual day of fasting and prayer. Hudson Taylor and his fellow workers lived in the spirit of prayer. This was a vital and abiding principle for the CIM and surely a reminder and a message for the worldwide Church today.

'The very existence of the China Inland Mission is a standing testimony, more forcible than words, to God's faithfulness in answer to prayer,' Hudson Taylor once wrote. 'The Misson was born of prayer, nourished by prayer, and is still sustained from month to month only in answer to believing prayer.'[15]

認為 Think

For James and Amelia Taylor, Hudson Taylor's parents, family prayer was 'a sacred institution'. They encouraged their children to believe in a God that listened to and answered prayer. History shows us that this instruction and role-modelling was significant. Surviving evidence – letters, sermons, written accounts in his own pen and, his life story – bear witness to Hudson Taylor's belief in the absolute necessity of prayer, for the most challenging of missionary endeavours through to the simplest of daily tasks. Looking back, we can see how God rewarded the prayerfulness and faithfulness of Hudson Taylor's parents, blessing them with a child who was to become one of the greatest missionaries the world has ever seen. Hudson Taylor's calling to China was born *of* prayer sustained *by* prayer, and fulfilled *through* prayer. Such is the importance and power of prayer.

響應 Respond

Hudson Taylor was a man called by God. He was called to discipleship but he was also called to an extraordinary mission, perhaps because he had offered himself to God in an extraordinary way. How many of us can honestly say that we have done as he did – prostrated ourselves before God in complete submission, offering our whole lives, everything we hold dear, to His service? If our children, our nation, our world, are to rediscover God and the power of the cross, perhaps more extraordinary offerings are required of us. So the question is not, 'Will we be called?' but rather, 'Do we *want* to be called?' 'Are we *willing* to be called?' 'Will we *ask* to be called?'

'Move men, through God, by prayer alone'

Chapter 3

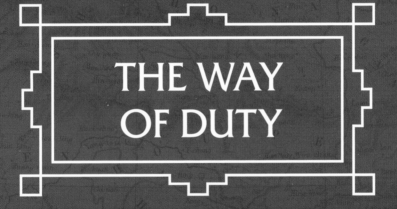

THE WAY OF DUTY

(1849–1853)

'An eminently practical turn'

"Come over and Help us."

A fac=simile of a scroll sent by two Chinese Converts as their appeal to British Christians.

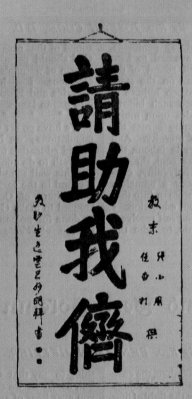

It pathetically re=echoes the old Macedonian cry "Come over and help us."

"WE PRAY YOU HELP US."

H udson Taylor's heart had been deeply moved by God prompting him to go to China, the land that he had already grown to love and care for with a passion way beyond his years. The clarity of this calling was such that there was no question about it. He was called to serve God in China, and that was what he would do.

So, though 'his emotional nature had been deeply moved' by the call, it also took with Hudson 'an eminently practical turn'.[1] If he was to go to China and tell the people there the message from God's Word, then there was work to be done in preparation. Hudson Taylor's commitment to his mission was immediate, focused and practical.

As much as Hudson already knew about China from the books and the stories of his childhood, there was now a great deal more knowledge he needed to absorb about his future home. So immediately, Hudson Taylor sought to become acquainted with, and prepare for, life in China. This meant acquiring more books on the subject.

Mr Whitworth (a local Sunday school superintendent and treasurer of the British and Foreign Bible Society) obtained for him a copy of Luke's Gospel in Mandarin; and a local congregational minister lent him a copy of W.H. Medhurst's *China: Its State and Prospects*.[2] The latter was devoured while the former, Luke's Gospel in Mandarin, was so diligently studied that in the space of just a few weeks Hudson had mastered over 500 Chinese characters.[3]

Alongside these, Mr Whitworth also provided Hudson Taylor with two magazines, *The Watchman* and *The Gleaner*, both of which enabled him to learn more about the various mission agencies at work in the world, including the newly formed organisation, The Chinese Association. Keen to start supporting any mission agencies with links to China, Hudson commenced a correspondence with George Pearse, the secretary of

Left:
Taken from a CIM publication, most likely *China's Millions*

In 1816, at just 20 years of age, Walter Medhurst set sail for Malacca to establish a printing facility for the London Missionary Society (LMS). In 1843, he became a pioneer for China, setting up the LMS mission centre in Shanghai. In 1854, he became the first chairperson of the Shanghai Municipal Council. He left China in 1856 due to ill health and died in England in January 1857. His epitaph reads, 'Forty Years a Missionary to the Chinese'. James Hudson Taylor worked alongside the Medhursts during his first few years in China, though they were not in Shanghai to greet Hudson Taylor when he first arrived there.

the association. This was to prove a providential connection, for just a few years later Hudson Taylor would sail to China as a missionary with this same association, by that time called the Chinese Evangelisation Society. Some of these letters to George Pearse still survive, giving us a very special insight into the mind of Hudson Taylor at that time. Unable to afford a language dictionary, his study of Mandarin had paused, so in one letter to Pearse, he explains his decision to study practical subjects such as anatomy, physiology, medicine and surgery: 'that I may have more opportunities of usefulness and perhaps be able to support myself when there'.[4]

In another letter Hudson responds to questions from George Pearse relating to his conversion, his God–given calling to China, and his suitability and readiness for the task ahead. Hudson's words as he recalls his conversion gives us real insight into the spirituality of the young man:

'Some of the reasons that make me think, nay, make me sure (for I have no doubt on the matter) that I am truly converted to God are as follows: the things I used formerly to delight in now give me no pleasure, while reading the Word, prayer and the means of grace, which were formerly distasteful to me, are now my delight. "Once the world was all my treasure And the world my heart possessed: Now I taste sublime pleasure Since the Lord has made me blest." I know that I have passed from death unto life because I love the brethren. The Spirit of God bears direct witness with my spirit that I am his child. My mind is kept in perfect peace because I trust in Him. And I feel no doubt that should I be called hence, when this earthly tabernacle is dissolved I have a building of God, a house not made with hands, eternal in the heavens. I feel I am but a stranger here. Heaven is my home.'[5]

Hudson Taylor's determination to study medicine led him to seek employment in a surgery, where he could acquire the necessary medical and surgical skills. As with everything, this need was submitted to God in prayer. His prayers were soon answered. Hudson Taylor's aunt (on his mother's side) was married to the brother of a Dr Robert Hardey of Hull, who owned a large general practice, had the surgical oversight of some factories and was a lecturer in the local School of Medicine. With Dr Hardey's help, a position was soon obtained for Hudson and once again, we see God's providence at work in the life of the aspiring doctor in training and future missionary to China. On 21 May 1851, his nineteenth birthday, Hudson commenced his new duties, and for the next 16 months Hull was to be his home.

Below:

Hudson Taylor's lodgings in Drainside, Hull

A disciplined life

When Hudson moved to Hull, he initially lived with his aunt, with the cost of his board provided by Dr Hardey. However, in order to be able to give his regular church offering, Hudson decided he should find cheaper lodgings. He acquired a bedsitting room in a humble cottage in Drainside, which cost him just three shillings a week. By practising very strict economies, he could now afford to give away as much as two thirds of his income. 'It was,' Marshall Broomhall observed, 'a school of simple and stern living, accompanied by many and varied blessings.'[6]

An insight into just how disciplined Hudson was about both his money and his diet is provided in a letter he wrote to his mother at this time. Not only do his words demonstrate his frugal approach, they reveal a man who was precise, accurate, and careful:

'I have found some brown biscuits which are really as cheap as bread, eighteen pence a stone, and much nicer. For breakfast I have biscuit and herring, which is cheaper than butter (three for a penny and half a one is enough) with coffee. For dinner I have at present a prune and apple pie. Prunes are two or three pence a pound and apples tenpence a peck. I use no sugar but loaf, which I powder, and at four pence halfpenny a pound I find it is cheaper than the coarser kind… I can get cheese at fourpence to sixpence a pound that is better than we often have at home for eightpence. Now I see rhubarb and lettuce in the market, so I shall soon have another change. I pickled a penny red cabbage with three halfpence worth of vinegar, which made me a large jarful. So you see, at little expense I enjoy many comforts.'

In his autobiography, Hudson reflected on the advice of his parents at that time. He was encouraged, he said, 'to use all the means in my power to develop the resources of body, mind, heart, and soul, and to wait prayerfully upon God.' This included a sacrificial approach to both his time and his possessions:

'I began to take more exercise in the open air to strengthen my physique. My feather bed I had taken away, and sought to dispense with as many other home comforts as I could, in order to prepare myself for rougher lines of life. I began also to do what Christian work was in my power, in the way of tract distribution, Sunday-School teaching, and visiting the poor and sick, as opportunity afforded.'[7]

'The effect of this blessed hope was a thoroughly practical one. It led me to look carefully through my little library to see if there were any books there that were not needed or likely to be of further service, and to examine my small wardrobe, to be quite sure that it contained nothing that I should be sorry to give account of should the Master come at once. The result was that the library was considerably diminished, to the benefit of some poor neighbours, and to the far greater benefit of my own soul, and that I found I had articles of clothing also which might be put to better advantage in other directions.'[8]

Hudson's spiritual life was also subject to discipline; prayer and Bible study were daily routines never to be missed. Such discipline ensured that faith was not at the mercy of feelings, so that when resolve weakened, as it sometimes did, habit prevailed. Hudson Taylor was determined to stay close to God, even during times of doubt or despair. The principle that to be a missionary abroad, you first had to prove yourself a missionary at home, he applied to himself, and later to those applying to work as missionaries in China through the China Inland Mission. Hudson also gave himself to evangelism, the 'awakening and converting work' he had witnessed as a child. His disciplined approach impacted his whole life; not one area was excluded. This proved vital preparation for his future work in China. The 'way of duty' was his determined choice but with it came many challenges for the still very young disciple – perhaps the hardest of all was the one that touched his heart.

'The way of duty is the way of safety'

Hudson Taylor was a young man looking forward to an uncertain life in a strange land. It was quite understandable, therefore, that the love and companionship of a wife would be naturally appealing. In December 1849, Hudson found himself falling in love with a friend of his sister, Amelia. It was a love that for some time he remained quiet about, telling only Amelia. Hudson was well aware of what would be required of his future wife. In his mind, not only was Miss V (as he refers to her in his letters to Amelia) an attractive and lovely young lady, she was a Christian, a Methodist, and 'so bright and gifted that he could not imagine her to be lacking in missionary devotion'.[9] The question that dominated his mind at this time was not about her suitability or willingness to travel, but rather how he could secure the means to support her.

Two years passed, and by now Hudson was living in Hull.

One cannot underestimate the challenges that Hudson was experiencing at this time: 'He was alone, hungry for love and sympathy, living a life of self-denial hard for a lad to bear.'[10] Then, sadly for Hudson, Miss V made it clear that she was not prepared to go to China after all. Her father would not permit it, and she herself did not feel fit for such a life and calling. The following extract from *Growth of a Soul* relates the agony that Hudson felt at this time, the conflict between human love and godly faith, and the very real temptations of the flesh and the world:

> '*Sunday morning came, December 14. It was cold and cheerless in the little room at Drainside. The lad was benumbed with sorrow, for instead of turning to the Lord for comfort he kept it to himself and nursed his grief. He did not want to pray. The trouble had come in between his soul and God. He could not, would not go as usual to the morning meeting. He was too full of bitter questionings and pain. Then came the cruel, insidious suggestion: "Is it all worthwhile? Why should you go to China? Why toil and suffer all your life for an ideal of duty? Give it up now, while you can yet win her. Earn a proper living like everybody else, and serve the Lord at home. For you can win her yet."*'[11]

This window into Hudson Taylor's private life reveals his humanity and his heart in a very personal way. Just because Hudson chose 'the way of duty' did not lessen the hardship of the sacrifice. But it was the love of God that prevailed at that moment, a love that enabled Hudson to sing for joy even while shedding tears of sorrow:

'*Well, on Sunday I felt no desire to go to the Meeting and was tempted very much. Satan seemed to come in as a flood and I was forced to cry: "Save, Lord; I perish." Still Satan suggested, "You never used to be tried as you have been lately. You cannot be in the right path, or God would help you and bless you more," and so on, until I felt inclined to give it all up. But, thank God, the way of duty is the way of safety. I went to the Meeting after all, as miserable as could be; but did not come away so. One hymn quite cut me to the heart. I was thankful that prayer followed, for I could not keep back my tears. But the load was lighter. Yes, He has humbled me and shown me what I was, revealing Himself as a present, a very present help in time of trouble. And though He does not deprive me of feeling in my trial, He enables me to sing, "Yet I will rejoice in the Lord, I will joy in the God of my salvation". Now I am happy in my Saviour's love. I can thank Him for all, even the most painful experiences of the past, and trust Him without fear for all that is to come.'* [12]

'Move man, through God, by prayer alone.'

The question of trust in Hudson Taylor's mind was not so much whether God was trustworthy: more whether his own faith was strong enough. During the winter of 1851-2, Hudson was contemplating life far away from home:

'It was for me a very grave matter, however, to contemplate going out to China, far away from all human aid, there to depend upon the living God alone for protection, supplies, and help of every kind. I felt that one's spiritual muscles required strengthening for such an undertaking. There was no doubt that if faith did not fail, God would not fail; but, then, what if one's faith should prove insufficient? I had not at that time learned that even "if we believe not, He abideth faithful, He cannot deny Himself", and it was consequently a very serious question to my mind, not whether He was faithful, but whether I had strong enough faith to warrant my embarking in the enterprise set before me. I thought to myself, "When I get to China, I shall have no claim on anyone for anything; my only claim will be on God. How important, therefore, to learn before leaving England to move man, through God, by prayer alone."' [13]

Hudson Taylor determined to put his faith to the test in a very simple and effective way. Hudson relied on his salary to pay all his monthly expenses – he had no reserves. So, he would not do what he usually did and remind his employer that his salary was due. Instead he would pray and leave God to do the reminding. He would tell no one what he was doing, but depend only on God. That way, any answers to prayer would be proved to have come from God alone.

When his next salary became due, Dr Hardey forgot, leaving his employee with just one half-crown piece, but Hudson continued to pray. That Sunday, with one coin left to his name, Hudson attended the morning service and afterwards visited the poorer areas of town, as was his custom. He was met by a poor man who begged Hudson to go with him and pray with his wife, who was dying. This poor couple and their children were also starving, leaving Hudson in a dilemma: he only had a little food at home to last until supper the next day, and all the money he had was in his pocket – in the form of just one coin. Had he possessed the same amount in a few coins he would gladly have given some away, but to give it all? Hudson was reluctant, but soon found himself handing over his last coin. The story continues in his own words:

'Not only was the poor woman's life saved, but I realized that my life was saved too! It might have been a wreck – would have been a wreck probably, as a Christian life – had not grace at that time conquered, and the striving of God's Spirit been obeyed. I well remember how that night, as I went home to my lodgings, my heart was as light as my pocket. The lonely, deserted streets resounded with a hymn of praise which I could not restrain. When I took my basin of gruel before retiring, I would not have exchanged it for a prince's feast. I reminded the Lord as I knelt at my bedside of His own Word that he who giveth to the poor, lendeth to the Lord: I asked Him not to let my loan be a long one, or I should have no dinner next day; and with peace within and peace without, I spent a happy, restful night.'[14]

Hudson's prayers were answered. The very next day Hudson received a letter containing a half sovereign. 'Praise the Lord', Hudson exclaimed, '400 per cent for twelve hours investment!' But the bigger problem still remained: Dr Hardey had not remembered the salary that was due to Hudson, and the young man would soon need to pay his rent. How easy it would have been for Hudson to remind him, but that would be to go back on his determination to 'move man, through God, by prayer alone'. Time passed and no salary was forthcoming. Hudson's prayers grew in earnest. It was a Saturday afternoon when Dr Hardey finally remembered. Hudson's heart leapt, only to fall dramatically when his employer told him that he had sent all the money to the bank. Downcast but not defeated, Hudson spent the afternoon in prayer and in the evening continued his usual duties, preparing gospel talks for the following day. A.J. Broomhall, Hudson Taylor's great nephew, completes the story:

'About ten pm Hudson packed up and put on his overcoat to go home. As he was going to put out the gaslight he heard Mr Hardey's footsteps on the garden path. He was chuckling, highly amused about something. At this late hour one of his wealthiest patients had come in to pay his bill. Hardey handed the cash to Hudson Taylor and Hudson went home praising the Lord "that after all I might go to China". "To me the incident was not a trivial one." It fully satisfied him that the principle was right, even small faith placed in a faithful God would always be honoured, and God was prepared to "move men" in answer to his children's prayers. Even on the other side of the world his needs would be supplied. This was better than dependence on human resources.'[15]

A 'simple, naked faith'

Above:
James Hudson
Taylor as a young
man, painted
by his aunt,
Hannah Hardey

After 16 months in Hull, Hudson Taylor sailed to London to continue his medical studies. His decision to go to London was another step of faith, for although he had lodgings to go to and money to pay for the hospital training fees, he had no suitable employment arranged. After just one month, though, he acquired a position at the London Hospital, but this entailed an eight-mile walk from his lodgings in Soho. This was an additional challenge for the young student, who was surviving on a very simple diet of brown bread and water, with the occasional apple. In a letter written at that time he admits to finding life difficult: 'Though the heavens have seemed as brass, and I have felt myself left and forsaken, I have been enabled to cling to the promises by simple, naked faith, as father calls it.'[16]

Here we see Hudson's 'godly heritage' at work. This 'simple, naked faith' was to prove a rock for Hudson on many an occasion in London. One episode, which left the young trainee doctor fighting for his life, powerfully demonstrates not only God's providential care for the man who had been called to serve God in China, but also Hudson Taylor's 'faith abounding'[17] and missionary zeal.

One November evening in 1852,[18] Hudson had been sewing together some sheets of paper on which to take notes of lectures, when he accidentally pricked the first finger of his right hand. He thought nothing of it, and the next day went to work at the hospital as usual, where he was dissecting the body of a person who had died from fever. It was a particularly dangerous dissection, and Hudson and his colleagues were very careful, knowing that the slightest scratch could cost them their life. When Hudson began to feel unwell he did not at first think of the needle prick from the night before. It only came to mind after speaking with the surgeon about his symptoms. 'Get a cab home immediately and put your affairs in order,' the surgeon told him. 'You are a dead man.'

'My first thought,' reflected Hudson Taylor, many years later, 'was one of sorrow that I could not go to China; but very soon came the feeling, 'Unless I am greatly mistaken, I have work to do in China and shall not die.' I was glad, however, to take the opportunity of speaking to my medical friend, who was a confirmed sceptic, of the joy that the prospect of soon being with my Master gave me, telling him at the same time that I did not think I should die, as unless I were much mistaken I had work to do in China, and if so, however severe the struggle, I must be brought through.'[19]

Hudson's 'simple, naked faith' in God was shown to be strong and he was indeed brought through. Not only that, but his basic diet proved fortuitous as the doctor told him in no uncertain terms, 'If you have been going in for beer and that sort of thing, there is no manner of chance for you.'[20] In the providence of God, Hudson's 'sober living' had helped save him. Once recovered, he visited the doctor who had treated him in order to settle the bill. He then proceeded to ask if he might speak freely to the doctor about his faith, which was duly allowed. At the end of their conversation the doctor concluded, with tears in his eye, 'I would give all the world for a faith like yours.'

When Hudson returned to London in January 1853, he learnt that the doctor had suffered a stroke and died. Hudson Taylor's recollection of their final conversation shows just how much this future missionary cared for souls everywhere: 'I cannot but entertain the hope that the

> The doctor had been sent to treat Hudson Taylor by Hudson Taylor's uncle, who had offered to pay all bills relating to his treatment and recovery – including supplies of port and 'as many chops as I could consume'! But Hudson felt that, once recovered, and with his own money, he should be the one to pay the doctor. However, the doctor refused to charge him as Hudson was just a student, which meant that Hudson had sufficient money to enable him to travel home to Barnsley. Hudson viewed this as 'a wonderful interposition of God on my behalf.'

Master Himself was speaking to him through His dealings with me, and that I shall meet him again in the Better Land. It would be no small joy to be welcomed by him when my own service is over.'[21]

Hudson Taylor continued his training in London, obtaining a post as a surgeon's assistant and living at St Mary Axe, Bishopsgate, within easy reach of the hospital and able, with his parents' help, to afford the comforts of home life. This proved a short but important period of spiritual and physical refreshment, a timely provision for the future missionary. By the end of the year he would be on a boat bound for China.

Reflection – Obedience

'Therefore go and make disciples of all nations, baptising them in the name of the Father and of the Son and of the Holy Spirit, and teaching them to obey everything I have commanded you. And surely I am with you always, to the very end of the age' *(Matthew 28:19–20)*

As Christians, we are all called by God to 'go and make disciples of all nations'; none of us are exempt. Hudson Taylor was as clear on this as he was about his own calling. His loyalty to Christ and the gospel made him unafraid to challenge people at home and abroad with Christ's call to evangelisation: 'When will it dawn on the Lord's people', he once said, 'that His command to preach the Gospel to every creature was not intended for the waste paper basket?' Hudson Taylor did not consider himself special for his calling. He was simply doing what Christ had commanded him to do, what Christ commands us *all* to do.

Hudson Taylor obeyed Christ's call. For him, it meant giving up the pleasures, the privileges and the comforts of life at home for service in a vast, strange and forgotten land. Not everyone will be called to such an extraordinary mission, but we are all called to mission, and as part of this call we must be prepared to make sacrifices, just as Hudson Taylor did. Obedience has a cost.

But obedience also brings confidence in a faithful God. To live according to God's will brings peace, power and safety, even in the most difficult and dangerous of circumstances. Hudson Taylor knew this and rested in it. A.J. Broomhall said of Hudson Taylor: 'In one confrontation or crisis after another the same undeviating determination is apparent. Once he knew what he should do, his action was decisive, whatever the opposition. Until then he would not move ahead of the will of God, however indecisive he might appear.'[22]

Hudson Taylor knew he must never allow dependence upon men to take the place of dependence upon God Himself. His incredible missionary endeavours were simply God working through him because he had submitted his life utterly and completely to the will of God. This is why Hudson Taylor was able to approach each task, even the seemingly impossible, with confidence. He had the courage to follow God not man, another principle that became an abiding practice of the China Inland Mission.

認為 Think

"'I never made a sacrifice", said Hudson Taylor in later years, looking back over a life in which to an unusual extent this element predominated. But what he said was true. For as in the case in point (his love for Miss V), the first great sacrifice he was privileged to make for China, the compensations that followed were so real and lasting that he came to see that giving up is inevitably receiving when one is dealing heart to heart with God.'[23]

Hudson Taylor demonstrated incredible obedience, strength and resolve as he prepared every area of his life for service in China. Physically, mentally, emotionally and spiritually, all areas were subject to the same discipline. Hudson called this 'the way of duty', an expression that might suggest it was something he had to do, rather than wanted to do. But that would be to misinterpret the man and the meaning. Even when the duty required significant sacrifice, Hudson was still able to praise God and approach his calling with joy. For Hudson Taylor, 'the way of duty' was not only 'the way of safety'; it was the way of peace, strength, courage, grace, even joy. He believed that before he left for China, and his life experience confirmed it. So, this is why, in later life, he could truthfully say that, 'I never made a sacrifice.'

響應 Respond

'I believe we are all in danger of accumulating – it may be from thoughtlessness, or from pressure of occupation – things which would be useful to others, while not needed by ourselves, and the retention of which entails loss of blessing. If the whole resources of the Church of God were well utilised, how much more might be accomplished! How many poor might be fed and naked clothed, and to how many of those as yet unreached the Gospel might be carried! Let me advise this line of things as a constant habit of mind, and a profitable course to be practically adopted whenever circumstances permit.'[24]

Consider Hudson Taylor's disciplined life. Dwell on the 'sacrificial living' that he demonstrated in his preparation for service in China, and on the words above. Is there something 'above and beyond' that you can do to show your love for God, for His world and for His people?

Chapter 4

A STRANGER IN A STRANGE LAND

(1853–1854)

*'For China's distant shore,
embark without delay. Behold
an open door, 'tis God that
leads the way.'*[1]

For China's Distant Shore.

1. For China's distant shore, Embark without delay;
1. Behold an open door: 'Tis God that leads the way.
1. His call is clear and loud; The missionary band
1. Should gather like a cloud, And leave their native land.

2. From friends and kindred go,
    By sense of duty led ;
The stranger and the foe
    To cherish in their stead.
'Tis hard to break each tie,
    But grace is freely given ;
And grace will strength supply
    When strongest ties are riven.

3. Away then, loved one, go
    When Jesus says, " Depart
Let nothing here below
    With Him divide thy heart.
He gave His all for thee :
    Leave all to serve thy Lord ;
And soon thine eyes shall see
    A hundredfold reward.

4. Away then, loved one, go,
    Whose spirit God has stirred ;
To stranger and to foe
    Convey the blessed word.
From friends and home away
    To China's distant shore ;
The sacred call obey,
    And hesitate no more.

5. The perils of the sea,
    The perils of the land,
Should not dishearten thee ;—
    Thy Lord is nigh at hand.
But should thy courage fail
    When tried and sorely pressed,
His promise will avail
    And set thy soul at rest.

6. Nor wilt thou grieve for home—
    The home that's left behind ;
The thought of one to come
    Will wholly fill thy mind.
And thou wilt bless the day
    When thou didst part with all,
And hasten far away
    At thy loved Master's call.

A t this time, mission in China was minimal, confined to five treaty ports where foreigners were allowed to reside and conduct trade. China, as we have already learnt, was generally considered 'a closed land', as penetration of the interior remained illegal and hazardous. The history of China, particularly in relation to government, Christianity and the presence of foreigners, is too complex to be covered in detail here. However, in order to appreciate the country as it was then, some understanding of the political situation and challenges that awaited Hudson Taylor is helpful.[2]

China 1850

A new emperor had just succeeded to the Dragon Throne, 19-year-old Xianfeng, already a widower with the reputation of being 'dissolute and spineless'. Immature and displaying signs of instability, the young emperor practised a particularly idolatrous and superstitious form of Buddhism. Christians, tolerated for a short while, were now labelled 'enemies of the public good' and once again lived with the threat of persecution. Open-air preaching in China was at best difficult, at worst impossible, and even mission hospitals were subject to threat. The Catholic Church were committed towards mission in China, but within the Protestant Church, particularly in Britain, interest was at a low ebb. The situation in China was 'compounded by the notorious failure of Charles Gutzlaff's Chinese Union'.

'Success,' wrote A. J. Broomhall, 'seemed as remote as ever.'[3] But events in China were about to take a more hopeful turn. The new Xianfeng Emperor had inherited two major problems: the assertive presence of foreigners on Chinese soil; and a rebellion in the hinterland of Canton

Charles Gutzlaff (1803–1851) was a German Lutheran Missionary, one of the first to go to China and to wear Chinese dress. He was involved in the first translation of the Bible into Chinese and was the founder of the Chinese Evangelisation Society that sent Hudson Taylor to China in 1853. Unfortunately, Gutzlaff was not a good administrator and his mission was beset with fraudsters: fake converts who, unbeknown to Gutzlaff, were actually opium addicts. Despite this, Hudson Taylor recognised Gutzlaff as foundational to Protestant Christian mission in China, calling him the 'grandfather of the China Inland Mission'.

by a sect known as the 'Worshippers of Shangdi', who had quasi-Christian beliefs. These 'Worshippers' had begun to resist the imperial Manchu (also known as Qing) government and were showing signs of developing into a serious menace. The seeds of the looming Taiping Rebellion (1850–1864) were being sown, a civil war that was to almost topple the imperial dynasty and at the same time pave the way for a more 'open door' to China.

China 1851–1853

By 1851, serious hostilities between the Manchu government, and the Taiping rebels, led by Hong Xiuquan, had escalated into what *The Times* newspaper in England reported as 'the greatest revolution the world has ever seen.'[4] Volunteers flocked to join the Taiping rebels against the unscrupulous imperial forces. As a result, a new Taiping dynasty – the Heavenly Kingdom of Great Peace – was formed, with Hong Xiuquan as its leader. A.J. Broomhall describes the cause for optimism for Christians worldwide over this development in China:

'They (the rebels) drew up a religious system of belief, codes of conduct, aims and objects. They would overthrow the Manchus, abolish idols, stamp out the opium vice and set up the kingdom of God in China. They honoured the Bible, gave prominence to the Ten Commandments, kept Saturday as the Lord's Day, used the Lord's Prayer, held daily meetings and two on the seventh day starting with the doxology and hymns in honour to the Triune God, read Scripture, recited a creed and listened to a sermon. And they baptised adults joining their ranks. Their moral code was in some ways strict: monogamy was for the ranks but concubines were permitted for leaders; opium smoking, drunkenness, theft and sacrifices to ancestors were forbidden. Idols were inexorably destroyed wherever they went. The poor were cared for and private property respected, in the early days. This was the reason for the excitement in the Christian world.'[5]

The Taipings made strong advances and by December 1852, they had entered Hunan Province, conquered a number of cities and seized vast military stores. Hong Xiuquan demonstrated his confidence in the rebellion by assuming the imperial title *Wan Sui* and using an emperor's seal. By March 1853 the rebels had captured Nanjing, the key to the Grand Canal – the main north-south waterway. In effect, China was now cut in half.

For foreigners in the Chinese treaty ports, and for the watching world, 'wishful speculation' abounded. They saw themselves 'on the threshold of an open empire... the whole country open to trade and travel.'[6] But while hope abounded, in reality the situation was incredibly volatile: trade almost came to a standstill; money was scarce as Chinese merchants packed up and fled; and allegiances became confused, for example when the secret society, the Triads, assumed the same name as the popular Taipings. Foreign adventurers began to serve as mercenaries in the Taiping, Triad or Manchu armies, with

Above:
Painting of conflict between Taipings and Manchus

foreign merchants supplying both sides with arms. Members of the Catholic Church, caught in the confused crossfire between the Manchus and the Taipings, were captured, killed or had their homes destroyed.

In June 1853, the Taiping rebels successfully crossed China's great Yellow River into Shanxi Province, which meant they were able to penetrate further east. The imperial court prepared to flee, leaving the feeble young Xianfeng Emperor praying to his gods for deliverance. A.J. Broomhall sums up the situation:

> 'The world held its breath. Manchu preparedness for such an emergency was negligible. Only a spontaneous emergence of sound generalship and loyalty could avert disaster. For too long, incompetence, corruption and sheer cowardice had been the marks of command in the imperial forces, while Taiping discipline, morals and the power of success carried them forward, against defences weakened by the terror their reputation inspired.'[7]

Shanghai 1853 – 'A mad-hatter world'

Above:
Shanghai
street scene

Politically, the situation in Shanghai was no less volatile than the situation in China generally. The walled city, built in 1554, had been seized by Taiping rebels in 1853. In September, that same year, the city fell to the Triads, or 'Red Turbans' as they were also known, though it was the imperial army of between 40–50,000 men surrounding the city that proved the greater source of concern to the foreign communities. To escape the war, many Chinese moved into settlements outside Shanghai, drastically increasing the

70

population and, in turn, the price of goods and property. Soon every available house was occupied and new buildings sprung up everywhere.

In many other ways, daily life in Shanghai was perfectly civilised and, until the fall of the city, trade had flourished. Inside the walled city were makeshift consulate and mission premises. Outside the walls, settlements for the British, French and American foreigners were laid out in blocks with intersecting roads. Business premises, residences, gardens and Chinese quarters were built, all with proper drainage. Horse-drawn carriages were used by the wealthy to get about the settlements, while others used sedan chairs, tartar ponies, hired coolies and even wheelbarrows (rickshaws were not invented until 1870). Chinese merchants and peasants accepted foreign rule on Chinese soil, and agreed to pay taxes in return for safety and security.

Below:
Town plan of Shanghai

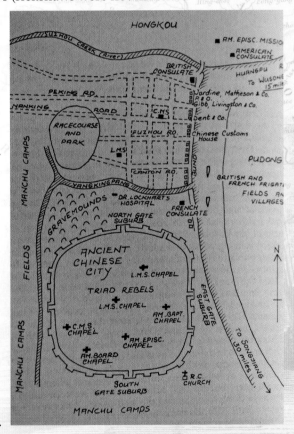

In 1845, the population of the Shanghai settlement numbered only about 90. Nine years later, however, the *Shanghai Almanac* listed 270 men, most of whom were aged between 19 and 35 years and worked as assistants in the merchant houses – some had families. In addition were hundreds of adventurers and seamen, who often outnumbered residents by as much as ten to one, and frequently caused havoc with their debauched and sometimes violent behaviour.

Opium trading increased even though banned by the Chinese government, and mortality rates were high. The community definitely had its own unique social problems.

Into this mix were the handful of missionaries who had stayed the course and continued with mission work throughout the rebel occupation. For example, the London Missionary Society had built a compound including homes and a chapel in the southwest corner of the settlement; inside the city walls they had two further preaching halls.

Missionary families assimilated into the culture and, as was expected of them, employed at least one cook, a watercarrier/outdoor man and a sewing woman ('aman') for the children. But they rarely attained high social status, being mainly viewed as 'social misfits'. Missionary ideals and morals were very much at odds with the merchant community, whose focus while living in China was 'self-indulgence and the rapid accumulation of wealth'.[8] Many of the unmarried merchants had their own 'kept' Chinese women, and gluttony abounded, no doubt contributing to the high mortality rate. The gulf further increased when the missionaries broke ranks by being classless among themselves and friendly with the Chinese. With the exception of 'the Christian and liberal elite on the one hand and the incontestably superior like Lockhart and Medhurst on the other',[9] this gulf was seldom bridged.

Hudson Taylor may have been 'in on the early evolution of what is now one of the largest cities in the world',[10] but the Shanghai that he was bound for when he set sail in the autumn of 1853 was 'a mad-hatter's world'.[11] Strange, confusing, highly volatile, dangerous – and a very long way from home.

From Liverpool to Shanghai

On Saturday afternoon, 4 June 1853, Hudson Taylor visited the London offices of the Chinese Evangelisation Society (CES), as he felt the time was right to realise God's call to China. Earlier that very same afternoon, Charles Bird, one of the secretaries of the society, had written to Hudson Taylor encouraging him to apply directly to CES for support to travel to China as a missionary. 'Do all with thy might, and speedily', it read. China's doors were opening, and Hudson Taylor was a man with the right personal, spiritual and practical credentials for mission work there. The letter lay on the desk, waiting to be posted, when in walked Hudson Taylor. Was this a mere coincidence, or was it a sign of God's leading? Both parties took it as providential proof; it was the confirmation Hudson Taylor was looking for. The following day Hudson wrote to his family asking for their advice and arrangements began to happen in a frenzy of activity. Departure was scheduled for September and gathering all he needed for the voyage as well as his new life as a missionary in China was a major task. And then there were important final visits to Hull and, of course, his beloved family in Barnsley.

Below:
Letter from Hudson Taylor to Benjamin Broomhall

Parting recollections

Hudson Taylor was to sail to China in a ship called *Dumfries*, which was due to sail from Liverpool early September. A number of delays meant that Hudson had time to track down his freighted medical equipment that had been delivered to the wrong address but, unfortunately, it meant that his father was not able to stay long enough to wave Hudson off. When *Dumfries* eventually set sail on 19 September 1853, his mother was the only member of his family on the dockside.

The last moments Hudson Taylor spent with his father and mother not only show the great heart of the young missionary, but they also depict the absolute agony experienced by this close-knit family at a parting they believed would be, in earthly terms, forever.

James Taylor – Father

'After waiting four days James Taylor could be away from his business no longer and they saw him off to Barnsley. Five years later Hudson still felt the agony of that parting from his father. It was traumatic, deeply etched in his memory. With a loud whistle and belching of smoke and steam the train began to move and gather speed. Hudson hung on and ran beside it, till it dragged them apart. Father and son looked long and hungrily into each other's faces in heartbreak and exultation together. They did not expect to meet again until 'in Glory'. But for Christ's sake and China's it was worth it.'[12]

Amelia Taylor – Mother
Hudson wrote in his autobiography:

'Never shall I forget that day, nor how she went with me into the little cabin that was to be my home for nearly six long months. With a mother's loving hand she smoothed the little bed. She sat by my side, and joined me in the last hymn that we would sing together before the long parting. We knelt down, and she prayed – the last mother's prayer I was to hear before starting for China. Then notice was given that we must separate, and we had to say goodbye, never expecting to meet on earth again. For my sake she restrained her feelings as much as possible. We parted; and she went on shore, giving me her blessing! I stood alone on deck, and she followed the ship as we moved towards the dock gates. As we passed through the gates, and the separation really commenced, I shall never forget the cry of anguish wrung from that mother's heart. It went through me

like a knife. I never knew so fully, until then, what 'God so loved the world' meant. And I am quite sure my precious mother learned more of the love of God to the perishing in that hour than in all her life before.'[13]

Amelia wrote:

> *'Then came my moment of trial – the farewell blessing, the parting embrace. A kind hand was extended from the shore. I stepped off the vessel, scarce knowing what I did, and was seated on a piece of timber lying close at hand. A chill came over me and I trembled from head to foot. But a warm arm was quickly around my neck and I was once more pressed to his loving breast. Seeing my distress he had leaped ashore to breathe words of consolation... As the vessel was receding he was obliged to return, and we lost sight of him for a minute. He had run to his cabin, and hastily writing in pencil on the blank leaf of a pocket Bible, "The love of God which passeth knowledge – J.H.T.", came back and threw it to me on the pier... While we still waved our handkerchiefs, watching the departing ship, he took his stand at its head and afterwards climbed into the rigging, waving his hat, and looking more like a victorious hero than a stripling just entering the battlefield. Then his figure became less and less distinct, and in a few minutes passenger and ship were lost to sight.'[14]*

'Even the winds and the waves obey him!' (Matthew 8:27)

The voyage from Liverpool to Shanghai was an eventful one. The *Dumfries* was a barque of 468 tonnes and three masts, and on board were 23 men: the captain, two shipmates, a steward, boatswain, cook and carpenter, nine able and two ordinary seamen, two boys and two apprentices, and just one passenger – James Hudson Taylor.

Captain Morris was a fellow Christian, and on more than one occasion during the voyage their shared faith, as well as Hudson's (albeit theoretical) knowledge of sailing[15] was to prove providential. The following accounts, both written by Hudson Taylor, demonstrate this:

Above:
Chinese sailing ship known as a junk

'Our voyage had a rough beginning, but many had promised to remember us in constant prayer. No small comfort was this; for we had scarcely left the Mersey when a violent equinoctial gale caught us... The gale steadily increased... until at last we were in a stone's throw of the rocks. About this time, as the ship, which had refused to stay, was put round in the other direction, the Christian captain said to me, "We cannot live half an hour: what of your call to China?" I had previously passed through a time of much conflict, but that was over, and it was a great joy to feel and to tell him that I would not for any consideration be in any other position; that I strongly expected to reach China; but that, if otherwise, at any rate the Master would say it was well that I was found seeking to obey His command!

'Within a few minutes after wearing ship the captain walked up to the compass, and said to me, "The wind has freed two points; we shall be able to beat out of the bay." And so we did. The bowsprit was sprung and the vessel seriously strained; but in a few days we got out to sea, and the necessary repairs were so thoroughly effected on board that our journey to China was in due time satisfactorily accomplished.'[16]

And then further on in the voyage:

'... a four knot current was carrying us rapidly towards some sunken reefs, and we were already so near that it seemed improbable that we should get through the afternoon in safety. After dinner the long boat was put out, and all hands endeavoured, without success, to turn the ship's head from the shore. After standing together on the deck for some time in silence, the captain said to me, "Well, we have done everything that can be done; we can only await the result." A thought occurred to me, and I replied, "No, there is one thing we have not done yet." "What is it?" he queried. "Four of us on board are Christians," I answered (the Swedish carpenter and our coloured steward, with the captain and myself); "let us each retire to his own cabin, and in agreed prayer ask the Lord to give us immediately a breeze. He can as easily send it now as at sunset."

'The captain complied with this proposal. I went and spoke to the other two men, and after prayer with the carpenter we all four retired to wait upon God. I had a good but very brief season in prayer, and then felt so satisfied that our request was granted that I could not continue asking, and very soon went up again on deck. The first officer, a godless man, was in charge. I went over to ask him to let down the clews or corners of the mainsail, which had been drawn up in order to lessen the useless flapping of the sail against the rigging. He answered, "What would be the good of that?" I told him we had been asking a wind from God, that it was coming immediately, and we were so near the reef by this time that there was not a minute to lose. With a look of incredulity and contempt, he said with an oath that he would rather see a wind than hear of it! But while he was speaking I watched his eye, and followed it up to the royal (the topmost sail), and there, sure enough, the corner of the sail was beginning to tremble in the coming breeze. "Don't you see the wind is coming? Look at the royal!" I exclaimed. "No, it is only a cat's paw," he rejoined (mere puff of wind). "Cat's paw or not," I cried, "pray let down the mainsail, and let us have the benefit!"

'This he was not slow to do. In another minute the heavy tread of the men on the deck brought up the captain from his cabin to see what was the matter; and he saw that the breeze had indeed come. In a few minutes we were plowing our way at six or seven knots an hour *through the water. We were soon out of danger; and though the wind was sometimes unsteady, we did not altogether lose it until after passing the Pelew Islands.*

'*Thus God encouraged me, ere landing on China's shores, to bring every variety of need to Him in prayer, and to expect that He would honour the name of the Lord Jesus, and give the help which each emergency required.*'[17]

The voyage was no doubt rich in experience for the young missionary. For five and a half months the *Dumfries* was his home, and during all this time he and the ship's company were cut off from the world outside, for the ship never touched land. The Cape of Good Hope was rounded in December, the nearest point to Australia was reached on 5 January, and the ship finally dropped anchor at Woosong, ten miles from Shanghai, on 1 March 1854.

Hudson Taylor had reached his destination. He was about to set foot in China, the land to which he had been called by God four years before. 'Through many dangers, toils and snares'[18] the young man had already come. But he could say, with growing confidence, 'Hold God's faithfulness'.[19]

Stepping ashore

Hudson Taylor's reflections as he approached, and then stepped onto, the land of China for the first time reveal his feelings the moment 'the dream of years' came true:

> '*"What peculiar feelings," wrote Hudson Taylor, as he waited for the boat to complete the final leg of the journey, "arise at the prospect of soon landing in an unknown country, in the midst of strangers – a country now to be my home and sphere of labour. 'Lo, I am with you always.' 'I will never leave thee nor forsake thee.' Sweet promises! I have nothing to fear with*

Jesus on my side. Great changes probably have taken place since last we heard from China. And what news shall I receive from England? Where shall I go, and how shall I live at first? These and a thousand other questions engage the mind".[20]

"'My feelings on stepping ashore," he wrote, "I cannot attempt to describe. My heart felt as though it had not room and must burst its bonds, while tears of gratitude and thankfulness fell from my eyes." Then a deep sense of the loneliness of his position came over him; not a friend or acquaintance anywhere; not a single hand held out to welcome him, or anyone who even knew his name. "Mingled with thankfulness for deliverance from many dangers and joy at finding myself at last on Chinese soil came a vivid realisation of the great distance between me and those I loved, and that I was a stranger in a strange land."'[21]

Below:
Shanghai port

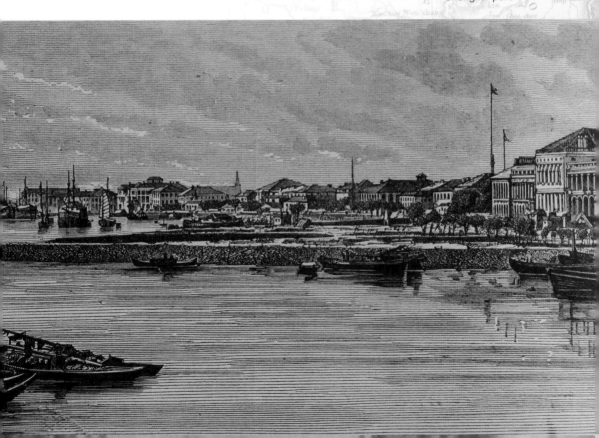

Hudson Taylor was just a young man, only 21 years of age, when he arrived in China, 'a stranger in a strange land'. This vast, spiritually needy land was now his home. Called by God, into the heart of 'the Dragon' – that strange, confusing, 'mad-hatter world' – Hudson Taylor now stood on the threshold of his longed-for missionary endeavour. This was the moment he had anticipated almost two years earlier. The moment when, he said, he would have 'no claim on anyone for anything; my only claim will be on God.' And he was right.

Reflection – Trust

'Trust in the LORD and do good; dwell in the land and enjoy safe pasture. Take delight in the LORD and he will give you the desires of your heart. Commit your way to the LORD; trust in Him and he will do this: he will make your righteous reward shine like the dawn, your vindication like the noonday sun' *(Psalm 37:3–6)*

Hudson Taylor had learnt to trust God at home. He had taught himself that God could be trusted by allowing himself to get in a position where his only claim was on God. 'How easy it is with money in the pocket and food in the cupboard to think that one has faith', he wrote. 'We need a faith that rests on a great God, and which expects Him to keep His own word and to do just what He has promised.'[22] Hudson's prayers – very private prayers – were answered. Only God knew his need; only God could have answered. He now knew that if he could trust God at home then he could trust God in China.

His belief in the abundance of divine resources enabled him to approach the work of the China Inland Mission (CIM) with the knowledge that 'God's work, done God's way, would not lack God's supplies'. To live within the will of God was to be sure that God would supply all that was needed for the fulfilment of His will. This was how and why Hudson Taylor could lead the CIM with such confidence. He did not lead in his own power, using his own resources. It was God-given power with God-given resources.

Hudson Taylor viewed *everything* as a gift from God. Mission funds were for mission; unnecessary personal funds were gifted for mission. He kept detailed public accounts. He practised a simple lifestyle: 'the bareness of the room... the well-worn dress of the man whose spirit seemed in such contrast with his surroundings', commented a prospective candidate for the CIM on visiting Hudson Taylor at his London home. And he exercised patience: 'It is not lost time to wait upon God'.

Hudson Taylor's calling required him to trust in God not just for his own life, but for the lives of all those who joined the CIM. This was an extraordinary mission *and* an extraordinary responsibility. But Hudson Taylor had learnt to trust God with no food in the cupboard and no money in his pocket; he knew first-hand what 'my only claim was on God' really meant. This was God's preparation for the incredible task ahead. Hudson Taylor could bear the burden of the CIM because he had learnt to trust in a living, all-powerful and infinitely faithful God.

認為 Think

'We dwell too much on the things that are seen and temporal', wrote Hudson Taylor to his sister Amelia in March 1852, 'and far too little on those that are unseen and eternal... Only let us keep these things in view, and the cares and the pleasures of this world will not affect us much... Oh, my dear Sister, let us live for eternity!'

Hudson Taylor was a stranger in a strange land. It was not just in China where he was a stranger; he saw himself as a foreigner and stranger on earth. God was his true home, eternity the vision he held before him. So, even amidst the very human agony of parting with his family, and the confusing, dangerous 'mad-hatter' world that he had stepped into, Hudson Taylor was still able to trust God and say to his sister with confidence, 'I will not fear what man shall do unto me'; and to his mother, 'The love of God which passeth knowledge'. Hudson Taylor had submitted his earthly life to God, knowing that there was eternity to look forward to. He had been set free from the ties that bind us here, released to live that truly abundant life that God promises those that give their lives to him.

響應 Respond

'The position of faith is incompatible with borrowing or going into debt or forcing our way forward when the Lord closes the door before us. If we propose a certain extension for which the Lord sees the time has not come, or which is not in accordance with His will, how can He more clearly guide us than by withholding the means? It would be a serious mistake, therefore, to refuse to listen to the Lord's "No" and by borrowing or going in to debt do the thing to which He had objected by withholding the needed funds or facilities. All the work we are engaged in is His rather than ours; and if the Master can afford to wait, surely the servant can also.'[23]

Trusting God is hard, even for the most practical things in life. We are taught to be responsible, to earn a living, to ensure that there is always 'money in the pocket and food in the cupboard'. And for most of us, most of the time, this is godly-living. But what if God calls you to a work, as He did Hudson Taylor and the workers of the CIM, which takes this 'normality' away? That calls you to trust in God for the very basics in life:

food, water, shelter? What about trusting God for friendships, fellowships and family? How would you respond then? We may not all be called to such depths of trust, but we should all be ready and willing.

> *'All God's giants have been weak men who did great things for God because they reckoned on God being with them.'*

Chapter 5

THE FIRST
SIX YEARS

(1854–1860)

'The valley of weeping'

When Hudson Taylor arrived in Shanghai, there was much for him to look forward to and do after the long and dangerous journey. He had mail to collect, a credit note from the Chinese Evangelisation Society (CES) awaiting him and letters of introduction to give to established missionaries and future colleagues – men with a shared heart for China. But then came the shock. The office that handled the mail had already closed for the day and two of his letters of introduction were useless (one of the intended recipients had died and the other had returned to the United States). Hudson was directed to the home of Walter Medhurst, one of the most prestigious people in the settlement at that time, and the intended recipient of his remaining letter of introduction. But Medhurst and his wife were away from the city, and their Chinese housekeeper was unable to help. His first day in China, and Hudson Taylor knew no one and had nowhere to go. His only hope was God – and God provided.

Before too long Hudson met a young Englishman from the London Missionary Society (LMS) named Joseph Edkins. He took Hudson to meet other missionaries including Dr William Lockhart, already established and fearless. Lockhart had arrived in Canton in 1838 and since then had worked and built hospitals in Macao, the Chusan Islands, Hong Kong and Shanghai. His wife, Catherine, was the first foreign woman to live in Shanghai. Lockhart made Hudson feel welcome, not only inviting him and other missionaries to dinner but also suggested that Hudson Taylor stay at his home for the present. One can only imagine his relief: 'I could hardly refrain from tears of joy when welcomed so cordially among them', wrote Hudson Taylor to his family in England, a couple of days later.

With no credit note forthcoming from the CES, Hudson was almost entirely dependent on the hospitality and generosity of Lockhart and the LMS, which, although happily given by his hosts, caused the young man great consternation. He was also unprepared for the distressing scenes he witnessed:

Right:
Letter from
Hudson Taylor
to Benjamin
Broomhall

'External hardships there were none, save the cold from which he suffered greatly; but distress of heart and mind seemed daily to increase. He could hardly look out of his window, much less take exercise in any direction, without witnessing misery such as he had never dreamed of before. The tortures inflicted by the soldiery of both armies upon unhappy prisoners from whom they hoped to extort money, and the ravages perpetrated as they pillaged the country for supplies, harrowed him unspeakably. And over all hung the dark pall of heathenism, weighing with a heavy oppression upon his spirit.'[1]

Then there was the continued absence of letters from home. Only one from his family awaited him on his arrival (though more had been sent), and time after time in the months that followed, Hudson would walk to the consulate to collect mail, only to be disappointed. It seemed that both friends and the CES decided to wait until he reached Shanghai before writing. 'Their inexperience and lack of imagination left him isolated, largely out of touch until July, four months after arrival in a strange land,' wrote A.J. Broomhall.

'My position is a very difficult one,' Hudson wrote in a letter to his parents, soon after his arrival. 'Dr Lockhart has taken me to reside with him for the present, as houses are not to be had for love or money... No one can live in the city, for they are fighting almost continuously. I see the walls from my window... and the firing is visible at night. They are fighting now, while I write, and the house shakes with the report of cannon. It is so cold that I can hardly think or hold the pen... You will see from my letter to Mr Pearse how perplexed I am. It will be four months before I can hear in reply, and the very kindness of the missionaries who have received me with open arms makes me fear to be burdensome. Jesus will guide me aright... I love the Chinese more than ever. Oh to be useful among them!'

Hudson Taylor was surely learning what 'my only claim will be on God' really meant.

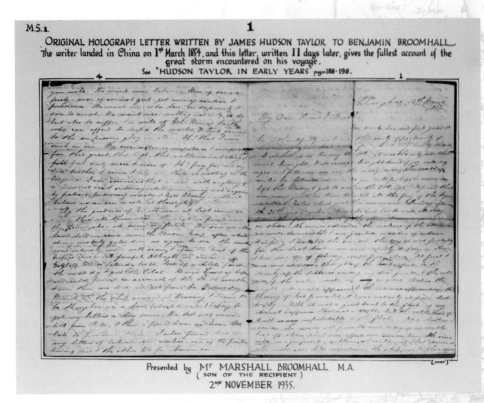

M.S.1.   **1**

ORIGINAL HOLOGRAPH LETTER WRITTEN BY JAMES HUDSON TAYLOR TO BENJAMIN BROOMHALL
The writer landed in China on 1ˢᵗ March 1854, and this letter, written 11 days later, gives the fullest account of the great storm encountered on his voyage.
See 'HUDSON TAYLOR IN EARLY YEARS' *pages* 188-198.

Presented by Mʳ MARSHALL BROOMHALL, M.A.
(SON OF THE RECIPIENT)
2ᴺᴰ NOVEMBER 1935.

'Man's extremity is God's opportunity': March 1854 – December 1855

There was more hardship to come for Hudson Taylor, experiences that were to prove themselves vital preparation for future missionary responsibilities. Spiritually speaking, Hudson was wise enough to understand the need for such preparation, but these were still hard lessons for a young missionary far away from his homeland, family and friends. Howard and Geraldine Taylor described the spiritual circumstance that Hudson found himself in:

> *'Until we are carried quite out of our depth, beyond all our own wisdom and resources, we are not more than beginners in the school of faith. Only as everything fails us and we fail ourselves, finding out how poor and weak we really are, how*

ignorant and helpless, do we begin to draw upon abiding strength... The Lord... makes His servant weak, puts him in circumstances that will shew him his own nothingness, that he may lean upon the strength that is unfailing. It is a long lesson for most of us; but it cannot be passed over until deeply learned. And God Himself thinks no trouble too great, no care too costly to teach us this.'[2]

Below:
Letter from
Hudson Taylor
to Amelia Taylor

Hudson Taylor's troubles at this time were indeed great: 'The horrors, atrocities, and misery connected with war'[3]; the extreme cold that exacerbated the practical challenges of life; the CES remained unforthcoming in their support; and then there was the intense loneliness. 'I feel the want of a companion very much', he wrote in the summer of 1854. Letters became especially important to the painfully alone young man, but even those sent were at the mercy of the winds and the waves, with many ending up either lost or delayed. 'Now your letters are very precious, you don't know how precious,' he wrote to his family. Amelia and his mother were faithful in this, as was Benjamin Broomhall, his close friend (and future brother-in-law), but we read that 'his father never wrote', and while other friends prayed faithfully, they 'seldom put pen to paper'.[4]

In all this, despite feeling humanly frail and at times at the point of despair – 'it needs strong faith to keep one's heart from sinking', he wrote in summer 1854 – Hudson Taylor's policy was always to advance. From his arrival in Shanghai in March 1854 through to December

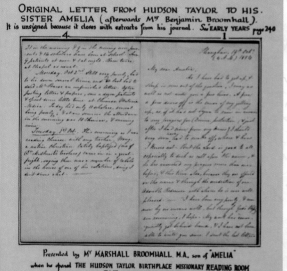

M.S. 2. 3

ORIGINAL LETTER FROM HUDSON TAYLOR TO HIS SISTER AMELIA (afterwards M⁀ Benjamin Broomhall). It is unsigned because it closes with extracts from his journal. See EARLY YEARS page 240

Presented by M⁀ MARSHALL BROOMHALL M.A. son of 'AMELIA' when he opened THE HUDSON TAYLOR BIRTHPLACE MISSIONARY READING ROOM 31ˢᵗ OCTOBER 1935.

A CHINESE ENVELOPE addressed by HUDSON TAYLOR to his sister 'AMELIA' Presented by M⁀ MARSHALL BROOMHALL. M.A. 2ᴺᴰ NOV. 1935.

1855, Hudson Taylor made many notable advances in the cause for Christ in China. A few of these early endeavours listed below give a flavour of the man whose 'faith abounding' and missionary zeal would one day see every province in China evangelised.

Sunday 5 March

Just four days after landing in China, Hudson and a fellow missionary, Alexander Wylie, climbed a ladder leaning against the city walls and spent the day chatting to the Triads and preaching the gospel.

Wednesday 8 March

Hudson had engaged the services of a Mandarin teacher on the advice of Walter Medhurst, and from then on spent six hours a day learning the language.

Sundays 19 and 26 March

Hudson joined Wylie on short excursions into the Chinese countryside, which taught Hudson vital early lessons in the challenges of travelling further inland.

August 1854

Hudson moved to a house just outside the north gate of the city to start his first main missionary endeavour: a school for children with times of Bible readings and prayers, a dispensary, and morning and evening prayers for the staff.

November 1854

Through necessity, Hudson moved back to the LMS compound in order to host a new CES missionary: Dr Parker and his family.

Below:
A Mandarin teacher

October, November and December 1854
Hudson Taylor and Dr Parker made many visits to towns and villages within a 15-mile radius of Shanghai, distributing 'more than eighteen hundred New Testaments and Scripture portions and two thousand two hundred Christian books and tracts'.[5]

December 1854 to March 1855
Hudson Taylor made his first four journeys inland, offering medical assistance ashore by day and engaging in evangelistic work at night. In this time he distributed a further 3,000 New Testaments, and 7,000 other books and tracts.

Above:
Moored junks

April 1855 to January 1856
Hudson Taylor made six further journeys into the interior. The sixth such journey, in May 1855, lasted 25 days and took him to 58 cities, towns and villages, 51 of which had never been visited by a Protestant missionary. The last journey was taken in the company of William Burns.

August 1855
Hudson Taylor commits to dressing in typical Chinese style, which involved dramatic changes to both clothes and hair: 'I resigned my locks to the barber, dyed my hair a good black,

and in the morning had a proper *queue* plaited in with my own, and a quantity of heavy silk to lengthen it out according to Chinese custom.'[6]

Such was Hudson Taylor's 'faith abounding' in the faithfulness of the almighty God, that even in the midst of the trials and challenges of these first months in China, he was able to stand firm and see God's guiding hand watching

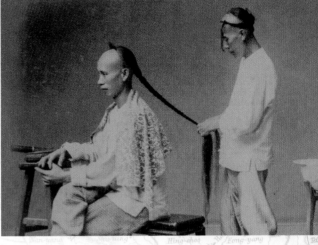

Above: Traditional Chinese dress and hairstyle

over him, believing that every circumstance was in some way a preparation for future work. 'Man's extremity is God's opportunity', he wrote in August 1855. Later, looking back with the eyes of understanding and the knowledge only time and hindsight enables, Hudson Taylor was able to reflect on these early days in China and to record, with confidence, how God's providential care shone through even the hardest of times:

'The cold, and even the hunger, the watchings and the sleeplessness of nights of danger, and the feeling at times of utter isolation and helplessness, were well and wisely chosen, and tenderly and lovingly meted out. What circumstances could have rendered the Word of God more sweet, the presence of God more real, the help of God more precious? They were times, indeed, of emptying and humbling, but were experiences that made not ashamed, and that strengthened purpose to go forward as God might direct, with his proved promise, "I will not fail thee, nor forsake thee". One can see, even now, that "as for God, His way is perfect", and yet can rejoice that the missionary path of today is comparatively a smooth and easy one.'[7]

'A place of springs'

'A long journey indeed through the Valley of Weeping; but oh, what springs of blessing! What rain filling the pools! We drink of it still today.'[8]

The Pilgrim's Progress by John Bunyan was read to him by his mother when he was a child, and was later to become part of the compulsory study programme for missionaries travelling to China with the China Inland Mission. William Burns first translated *The Pilgrim's Progress* into Chinese.

In *The Pilgrim's Progress*, a book very dear to Hudson Taylor, the pilgrim Christian has to climb the 'Hill Difficulty', before arriving at the 'palace Beautiful' – a place of physical and spiritual rest and renewal. Hudson Taylor would no doubt have identified with Christian as he climbed his own 'Hill Difficulty' in those early days in China. How he must have longed for that precious 'palace Beautiful' to appear, with its attendant blessings of spiritual fellowship.

Despite the generous hospitality and support of the LMS missionaries (which he never forgot), Hudson Taylor still felt very alone. What he really craved was the close companionship of a spiritual soulmate, and a wife.

William Burns (1815–1868): 'A spiritual father'

In July 1855, Hudson Taylor wrote these words in a letter to his parents: 'I do long for a helpful companion with whom I could take counsel and have real sympathy of mind and feeling, and to be fixed somewhere in good, regular work.' In just a few months, the first of these prayers was to be answered, in the form of the apostolic missionary, William Burns. Burns' wide experience as an evangelist in Scotland, Canada and in China made him just the friend and counsellor that Hudson Taylor had so desperately longed for. A very strong, God-centred and mission-focused friendship soon developed between the two men. 'I had never had such a spiritual father as Mr Burns; I have never known such holy, happy fellowship,' reflected Hudson Taylor many years later.[9]

In December 1854, not long after they had met, Burns accompanied Hudson Taylor on his tenth evangelistic journey. On their return, both men separately sensed God's call to Shantou, a busy, important and populous port south of Shanghai and Ningbo. The notorious centre of the opium trade, Shantou was a place of violence and vice, inhabited by foreigners but without any missionary presence. In March 1856, heeding God's call, Hudson Taylor and William Burns sailed together to take the message of Christ to the people of Shantou. It was to prove a difficult few months, testing the two missionaries to their limits. Hudson Taylor described it as 'such a wicked place', requiring 'far more faith and self-denial than anything I have ever known… the hatred and contempt of the Cantonese was very painful… but all this led us into deeper fellowship than I had ever known before with Him who was 'despised and rejected of men'.[10]

Their time together in Shantou was to be only a brief interlude, however. The dark clouds of war were looming, and Hudson Taylor was needed, temporarily they thought, back in Shanghai. But circumstance dictated that the two men would not meet

Below:
Map showing Swatow (also known as Shantou)

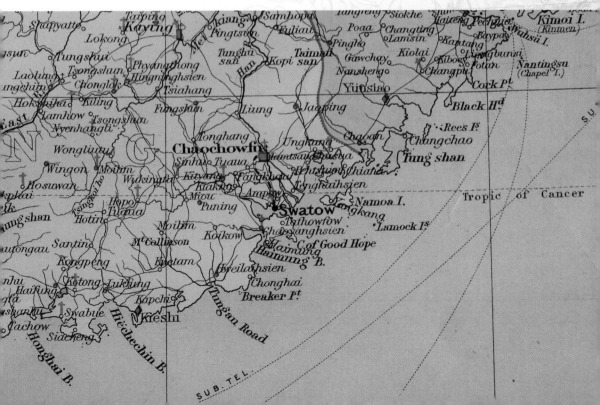

again on earth. Their season of friendship and shared mission was just a very brief one, but it was still hugely significant, timely and never to be forgotten. 'Those happy months were an unspeakable joy and privilege to me,' wrote Hudson Taylor in his autobiography. 'His love for the Word was delightful, and his holy, reverential life and constant communings with God made fellowship with him satisfying with the deep cravings of my heart. His accounts of revival work and of persecutions in Canada, and Dublin, and in Southern China were most instructive, as well as interesting; for with true spiritual insight he often pointed out God's purposes in trial in a way that made all life assume quite a new aspect and value. His views especially about evangelism as the great work of the Church, and the order of lay evangelists as a lost order that Scripture required to be restored, were seed-thoughts which were to prove fruitful in the subsequent organization of the China Inland Mission.'

Maria and her sister Burella were daughters of Rev Samuel Dyer, himself dedicated to mission work among the Chinese. Until his death in 1843, Samuel Dyer spent 16 years in service with the London Missionary Society (LMS), based mainly in Malacca at the China headquarters of the LMS, and in Singapore. His three children all succeeded him in mission work for China. Maria was just six years old when her father died, and ten when her mother died. The Dyer children were left in the care of an uncle, Mr Tarn, in London.

Maria Dyer (1837–1870): 'An inestimable prize'

Hudson Taylor felt the absence of a wife particularly keenly. He had lost his first love, and now the situation seemed bleaker than ever. In a letter to his mother in June 1854, Hudson Taylor wrote openly and honestly about his need and desire for what he described as 'an inestimable prize'. At that time, far away from home and with very small missionary communities, the prospect of finding a suitable wife seemed very remote, if not impossible. It was a situation in which he really struggled to trust God. 'I am a dull scholar and slow to learn to leave myself *altogether* in His hand,' he confessed in the letter to his mother. But the promise that was to become so dear to Hudson Taylor: 'If we believe not, yet he abideth faithful; he cannot deny himself' (2 Timothy 2:13, AKJV) held firm in this situation, as in many. God's plan for Hudson Taylor did include a wife, but it was to be *His* chosen wife in *His* intended – and perfect – time. It was October 1856 and Hudson Taylor was stationed in Ningbo, a port just south of Shanghai. Maria Dyer was a young girl, just 19 years of age, working at a school for girls in Ningbo, the first of its kind to be opened by missionaries in China.

Hudson and Maria met on a number of occasions at the house of a mutual friend. They had much in common, especially their love for God and for China, and soon 'she began to fill a place in his heart never filled before'. Although longing for a wife and home, Hudson was deeply conscious of his call to the interior of China, a life which might be easier undertaken without any responsibilities. Added to this, he had no financial means to support a wife, and so he did all he could to banish her image from his mind.

Above: Maria and Hudson Taylor

Then, in November of that year, news came that England was at war with China. By January 1857, the situation was serious enough to effect the removal of the foreign community to the safer port area of Shanghai. Hudson Taylor was called back from Shantou as he was needed to help escort the foreigners to Shanghai, which would be his home once again for the next five months. During this time several events happened: Burns wrote that he had a new colleague working with him in Shantou, confirming to Hudson that God had closed that particular door; in early spring, he learnt of the engagement of his sister Amelia to his good friend Benjamin Broomhall; and in May, just before his return to Ningbo, Hudson took the difficult decision to resign from the CES.

At the same time, never far from Hudson's thoughts, was his unresolved relationship with Maria Dyer, which circumstance seemed to be conspiring against.

Everything seemed to be preventing their mutual love from flourishing: Hudson Taylor's situation and calling; war between England and China; his subsequent removal from Ningbo to Shanghai; the animosity towards him from Miss Aldersley (the lady in charge of the school where Maria worked, and her guardian in China); and, most heart-breaking of all, a letter from Maria to Hudson, dismissing all possibility of marriage. When Hudson returned to work in Ningbo in May 1857, he had little hope of a future with the woman he had met there, and fallen in love with, some months before.

However, soon events began to take a more hopeful turn. An opportunity for them to meet was arranged by supportive friends and it was here that Hudson and Maria publicly declared their love for each other and submission to God's calling. All that was needed now was consent to the marriage from Maria's uncle in London. In November 1857, after months of painful waiting, the happy news arrived that they had been longing for – permission was granted. Four days after Maria's twenty-first birthday, on 20 January 1858, Hudson Taylor and Maria Dyer were joined together in holy matrimony. The ceremony took place in an old Chinese temple; Hudson Taylor wore his Chinese robes, and Maria Dyer a simple grey silk gown. Hudson had finally received that long-awaited 'inestimable prize' and he was not disappointed:

> The Chinese Evangelisation Society was finally dissolved in the summer of 1860, with the final edition of *The Gleaner* issued in September 1860. With no denominational church behind it, inadequate donations, and costs far beyond expectation, it became impossible to continue. The decision was not disputed by its supporters.

'Oh, to be married to the one you do love, and love most tenderly. This is bliss beyond the power of words to express or imagination to conceive. There is no disappointment there. And every day it shows

more of the mind of your Beloved, when you have such a treasure as mine, makes you only more proud, more happy, more humbly thankful to the Giver of all good for this best of all earthly gifts.'[11]

'Enchanted ground'

'My soul is not at rest. There comes a strange and secret whisper to my... spirit, like a dream of night, that tells me I am on enchanted ground.'[12]

In Hudson Taylor's own words, to walk with God is to be on 'enchanted ground'. For the next two and a half years Hudson and Maria Taylor were tireless workers for the cause of Christ in China. 'Perhaps', wrote Hudson Taylor, 'if there were more of the intense distress for souls that leads to tears, we should more frequently see the results we desire... How much of the precious time and strength of our Lord was spent in conferring temporal blessings on the poor, the afflicted and the needy. Such ministrations, proceeding from right motives, cannot be lost. They are Godlike, they are Christlike.'[13] Their home was a small Chinese house on Bridge Street, Ningbo; their work a mixture of evangelisation and faith in action. 'By word and by deed,' recalled Marshall Broomhall, 'they followed in the footsteps of Him who went about doing good.'

Below: Maria and Hudson Taylor's home in Bridge Street, Ningbo

This was a very happy and blessed time for the young couple, but not without its challenges. In February 1859, Maria became so seriously ill that Hudson feared for her life. But God was able and willing to heal and, miraculously, Maria survived – 'the Great Physician Himself had been present

and done the work'. 'Such experiences of Divine intervention,' reflected Marshall Broomhall, 'make the unseen real. Life can never again be quite the same.'[14] Just a few months later, on 31 July 1859, the couple were blessed with the birth of their first-born child, Gracie. A 'Valley of Weeping' had been replaced by a 'Place of Springs'.

But there were further challenges ahead for Hudson and Maria. Great Britain was at war with China and missionaries were seen, by some, in the same light as British government officials. This meant that the lives and property of the small European community in Ningbo were in grave danger from certain Chinese people out for revenge. The fierce summer heat was taking its toll, and in August of that year the wife of Dr Parker, the only medical man in Ningbo, died, leaving him with four children and no choice but to leave China and return home to Scotland. Out of necessity, Hudson Taylor felt constrained to take on full responsibility for both the hospital and the dispensary – to close either would be to doubt God and his faithfulness in provision – but this was a huge undertaking both practically and financially. The expenses of the hospital and dispensary had been met by Dr Parker's European practices. When he left, this support ended, included the guaranteed salaries of the staff.

Hudson Taylor may not have been prepared for such an unexpected turn of events, but God was. 'Before they call I will answer', reads Isaiah 65:24. Provision was already in hand, in the form of a letter from William Berger in England, with a cheque for £50 and the pledge of more using an inheritance, which was surplus to his needs. Other gifts and spiritual blessings followed: 16 patients were baptised and more than 30 others enrolled as candidates for baptism.

The constant physical and mental strain of the work on Hudson began to endanger his health, however, and reluctantly he had to admit that they could no longer carry such a huge burden alone. They desperately needed rest and recovery. So

Right:
Wang Lae-Djun

with heavy hearts, the hospital in Ningbo was closed. In June 1860, the Taylors moved back to Shanghai, and in July they sailed for home aboard the ship *Jubilee*. Wang Lae-Djun, a Chinese Christian, went with them to assist with language work in England.

When Hudson Taylor stepped ashore in England four months later, with his wife Maria and daughter Gracie by his side, he did not know if he would see his beloved China again. The future was 'a ravelled maze' and all Hudson knew was the immediate next step and the desire that God had planted in his heart for China. This was how he had learnt to live for Christ. It was one step at a time in the direction of God's call, with the knowledge and assurance that each step was 'on enchanted ground'.

Reflection – Sacrifice and suffering

'But he said to me, "My grace is sufficient for you, for my power is made perfect in weakness." Therefore I will boast all the more gladly about my weaknesses, so that Christ's power might rest on me. That is why, for Christ's sake, I delight in weaknesses, in insults, in hardships, in persecutions, in difficulties. For when I am weak, then I am strong.' *(2 Corinthians 12:9–10)*

Intense suffering and sacrifice would become an intrinsic part of Hudson Taylor's life story and that of the China Inland

Mission (CIM). Christ Jesus was his Lord, his Saviour *and* his example. Just as Christ had suffered, so Hudson Taylor expected to suffer too. He knew that a life of service would be a challenging one, with more than one 'Hill Difficulty' and 'Valley of Weeping'. But serving Christ with this knowledge did not lessen the impact or make it any easier. Hudson Taylor was a man with a deep love for humanity: a vast capacity for care, compassion and service – often to the detriment of his own health and well-being. When others suffered he felt their pain, and wherever and whenever he could, he would be on hand to help. He made it a principle that as leader he would not ask of anyone what he was not prepared to do himself. He believed that a call to serve was a call to lay *everything* at the altar, and as leader of the CIM, it was his responsibility to set an example.

It was an example of practice and of response. It was not just how Hudson Taylor acted in adversity, but his attitude towards it also, that formed the model for the CIM. It was Hudson Taylor's spiritual response to suffering that enabled him to cope with it on a human level. 'The wise and trustful child of God rejoices in tribulation,' he said. To suffer for Christ was an honour. He understood that such experiences drew one closer to God and built character, compassion, strength and understanding in a way nothing else could. This was why in later years he could write on the subject of suffering and call it 'Blessed Adversity'; and say, with complete conviction, 'I never made a sacrifice.'

認為 Think

'Who spoke of rest? There is rest above.
No rest on earth for me. On, on to do
My Father's business. He, who sent me here,
Appointed me my time on earth to bide.
And set me all my work to do for Him,
He will supply me with sufficient grace –
Grace to be doing, to be suffering,
Not to be resting. There is rest above.'[15]

Hudson Taylor and the workers of the CIM laid down their lives for the cause for Christ in China. Nothing was too much to bear for their Lord and Saviour. Many lived long and fulfilling lives and saw significant fruit for their labours, but most suffered personally through illness, separation or bereavement and many lost their lives in service, including the 58 missionaries and 21 children who were tragically martyred during the Boxer Rebellion in 1900.

Christ suffered and died that we might live. To strive to be Christlike is to be prepared to live like Christ. We must be prepared to face rejection, scorn and sorrow in order to live lives 'set apart': to take up *our cross* and follow Him. What are you prepared to sacrifice or suffer for the cause for Christ in our world today?

響應 Respond

'Speaking to my students one day, I asked them: "Young men,
which is the longest, widest and most populous valley in the
world?" And they began to summon up all their geographical
information to answer me. But it was not the valley of the
Yangtze, the Congo, or the Mississippi. Nay, this Jammerthal,
as it is in our German, this valley of Baca, or weeping, exceeds
them all. For six thousand years we trace it back, filled all the
way with an innumerable multitude. For every life passes at

some time into the Vale of Weeping. But the point for us is not what do we suffer here, but what do we leave behind us? What have we made of it, this long, dark, Valley, for ourselves and others? What is our attitude as we pass through its shadows? Do we desire only, chiefly, the shortest way out? Or do we seek to find it, to make it, according to his Promise, "a place of springs": here a spring and there a spring, for the blessing of others and the glory of our God?"[16]

Consider the questions contained in the words above. Reflect on your response to sacrifice and suffering. Do you seek for a way to escape any personal discomfort or suffering? Or will you seek to make it 'a place of springs' for the blessing of others and the glory of our God?

'Man's extremity is God's opportunity.'

Chapter 6

A TWO-FOLD
VISION

(1860–1865)

God and China

1862

JAMES HUDSON TAYLOR
AFTER HIS FIRST PERIOD
OF SERVICE IN CHINA

1862

MRS. HUDSON TAYLOR,
(NEE MARIA DYER.)
THEY WERE MARRIED IN 1858.

The Taylor family arrived in London on 28 November 1860, where they briefly settled in the Bayswater home of Benjamin and Amelia Broomhall. That Christmas was spent enjoying a family reunion in Barnsley with Hudson's beloved parents, his younger sister Louisa, Amelia and Benjamin Broomhall, and Hannah and Richard Hardey (his aunt and uncle from Hull).[1] Hudson's health – particularly his liver, digestion and nervous system – was seriously impaired; years of good climate and healthy diet were required to sufficiently recover. A future back in China seemed at best uncertain and at worst impossible.

So, five months after their arrival in England, the Taylors rented 1 Beaumont Street, a small house in the East End of London close to the London Hospital where he had trained in medicine. It was some comfort to Hudson that he could still serve China from his home in the East End. As well as getting some much-needed rest and refreshment, time at home was an opportunity for finding fellow labourers and fitting himself for future usefulness. Hudson Taylor's policy of 'advance' was as relevant in England as it was in China.

These years proved to be a time of great personal and spiritual blessing for Hudson Taylor and Maria in the form of new and deepening friendships, a wider circle of partners in mission and prayer, improved health, and time with his beloved, growing family. Children born during this time in England included Herbert in April 1861, Frederick (who was later known as Howard) in November 1862, Samuel in June 1864 and Jane Dyer who was born but sadly died soon after in December 1865. This was a season of God's providential care and vital preparation for future work, an 'unforeseen ministry' greater than anyone at that time envisaged – including Hudson.

It was also a period for focused consolidation and reflection as Hudson's heart and mind were never far from China. Much had been experienced in the seven years away from home: heights of happiness, depths of despair, intense loneliness and extremes of culture, comfort and climate. On more than one occasion he had come face to face with death. Hudson Taylor was now a much more mature man – physically, practically, emotionally and spiritually. Important foundations had been laid for future work; knowledge had to be utilised, and resources deployed. Hudson may have aged considerably in health and appearance but his 'faith abounding' and missionary zeal were just as strong, if not stronger than ever.

Hudson Taylor had formed a particular attachment to the small community in Ningbo and it was to them he initially longed to return. With poor health, a role at Ningbo must have seemed both a sensible and realistic option. But God was calling him to the inland provinces and the vast unreached populations that had touched his heart from childhood. 'China's Millions' became an increasing burden to the recuperating missionary, with no clear solution as to how he could help given his limited capacity.[2] But as Hudson studied God's Word and daily viewed the large map of China on his study wall, 'a two-fold vision' gradually dawned on him: 'with the deeper sense of China's need came the fuller realization of Divine Resources.'[3] 'Our Father is a very experienced One,' he once wrote. 'He knows very well that His children wake up with a good appetite every morning, and He always provides breakfast for them, and does not send them supperless to bed at night. "Thy bread shall be given thee, and thy water shall be sure."'[4]

A mission to China was a partnership with God: a God who could, and would, provide. This gave Hudson Taylor a new-found confidence, and from that moment on he knew he could venture all for China with the assurance that 'if God were with him, and for him, it did not matter who, or what, was against him.'[5] He could depend upon it. He could act upon it. God would provide.

Preparations to return to China

With renewed passion, combined with a sense of responsibility, Hudson Taylor committed to preparing himself and others for the evangelisation of China. Early in 1861, he and Maria became members of Westbourne Grove Chapel, and for the first time he agreed to be addressed as 'Reverend'. In the spring, he enrolled at the London Hospital to complete his medical training, and by October 1862 had qualified as both doctor and midwife. Hudson was well aware that formalising the roles of both minister and doctor would be hugely beneficial to future missionary work in China.

Alongside his medical training, Hudson was engaged in translation work. With the small community at Ningbo never far from his thoughts and prayers, his first project was a hymn book in the Ningbo dialect, which went to press in March 1861. This left Hudson time and energy to spend on the revision of the Ningbo New Testament with the help of his friend, Rev F.F. Gough. This was to be a long and often fraught exercise, due mainly to uncertainty regarding vital support from the Bible Society combined with not infrequent tensions between the two translators.[6]

In addition, Hudson was doing all he could to broadcast the need for mission workers in China: writing articles for magazines, preaching and speaking and appealing to mission societies. Hudson was certainly not idle; in his journal for January–April 1863, he records his daily activities, including the many hours spent in translation work and proofreading.[7] His evenings were generally spent in prayer, at meetings, at preaching engagements and in letter writing. He was also writing, in quite incredible detail, his vision for China in a booklet called *China: Its Spiritual Needs and Claims*. Commenced in January and published in October 1865, it combined history and facts to form an irresistible argument for mission work in China, as well as proving to be instrumental in the dissemination of knowledge, and in the recruitment of missionaries to China. All this, while still suffering from poor health, gives an indication of Hudson's commitment to 'China's Millions'.

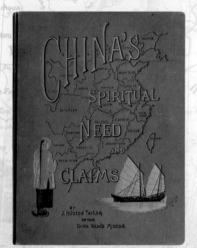

As a couple, Hudson Taylor and Maria were heavily involved in supporting candidates for mission work, many of whom went to live with them in their home in the East End. James Meadows, who sailed for China in January 1862, was one such missionary. Howard and Geraldine Taylor's description offers a glimpse into the Taylor home at this time: the young man, on his arrival, was surprised at 'the poverty of the little house', the 'bareness of the room' and 'the well-worn dress of the man whose spirit seemed in contrast with his surroundings'. But the 'simple earnest piety' of the small company meant that Meadows was surprised to find himself 'unruffled by things that would have upset his peace of mind at home'.[8]

Many others were made welcome by the Taylors, meaning that by September 1864, a move to a larger residence in Coborn Street, East London was necessary, the additional rent paid by

Rev Gough. Such was the Taylors' devotion to the cause that their home became the informal headquarters for mission activity and the growing vision for China.[9]

Above: 69 Coborn Street, London

A deepening relationship with God

'I have often seen since,' wrote Hudson Taylor many years later, 'that, without those months of feeding and feasting on the Word of God, I should have been quite unprepared to form, on its present basis, a mission like the China Inland Mission.'[10]

This 'feeding and feasting' was primarily referring to the hours Hudson spent daily working on the revision of the Ningbo New Testament. This required huge concentration of thought, 'more than many strong men could endure'; but it also enabled Hudson Taylor to spend hours meditating on 'the value and significance of words' – God's Words.[11] Those hours of study must have powerfully impacted Hudson Taylor as he considered each and every word of the New Testament for the benefit of the Ningbo people. God was surely speaking to Hudson through this work; the two-fold vision – God and China – ever before his eyes.

As he studied and read, strategies that were to prove foundational to the China Inland Mission were unveiled, and God-centred practices and principles of mission were clarified:

> 'In the study of that Divine Word I learned that to obtain successful labourers, not elaborate appeals for help, but, first, earnest prayer to God to thrust forth labourers, and second, the deepening of the spiritual life of the Church, so that men should be unable to stay at home, were what was needed. I saw that the Apostolic plan was not to raise ways and means, but to go and do the work, trusting in his sure word who had said, "Seek ye first the Kingdom of God and His righteousness, and all these things shall be added unto you."'[12]

Prayer to the almighty, faithful and *living* God became the life-blood of Hudson Taylor's great co-mission. He had seen God answer prayer in incredible ways, and as he dwelt more deeply in God's Word he came to see the power and importance of prayer as absolutely foundational to all mission activity. This became a principle and a practice from which he never swerved, and it stemmed from an unshakeable belief in the faithfulness of God:

> *'The Word had said: "Seek first the Kingdom of God and His righteousness, and all these things (food and raiment) shall be added unto you." If anyone did not believe that God spoke the truth, it would be better for him not to go to China to propagate the faith. If he did believe it, surely the promise sufficed. Again, "no good thing will He withhold from them that walk uprightly". If anyone did not mean to walk uprightly he had better stay at home. If he did mean to walk uprightly, he had all he needed in the shape of a guarantee fund. God owns all the silver and the gold in the world, and the cattle on a thousand hills. We need not be vegetarians!'[13]*

More and more, Hudson Taylor was conscious that if he lived in God, there was nothing that could not be done 'He sustained three million Israelites in the wilderness for forty years. We do not expect He will send three million missionaries to China; but if He did, He would have ample means to sustain them all. Let us see that we keep God before our eyes; that we walk in His ways and seek to please and glorify Him in everything, great and small. Depend upon it, God's work done in God's way will never lack God's supplies.'[14]

Hudson Taylor believed in God, and he believed implicitly in God's Word. God to him was real, His Word was real, and the needs of the world were real. And so were 'Divine Resources'. Hudson had known this before he went to China, but these years detained in England were revealing it in a new, dynamic and vital way. He was learning to see his passion for China as a practical partnership with a God who was all-powerful, mighty, loving and infinitely faithful.

> 'God was becoming all in all to him. God was not a God afar off, but nigh at hand. God was his Father and he His child, and the childlike spirit became his strength. "Have faith in God" meant more and more as years rolled by. He learned to "lean more constantly, to draw more largely, to rest more implicitly, on the strength, the riches, and the fullness" of God in Christ. And one verse which he frequently inscribed in people's birthday books, or autograph albums, was: "The Lord thy God is in the midst of thee, a Mighty One who will save; He will rejoice over thee with joy, He will rest in His love, He will joy over thee with singing." And the joy of the Lord became his strength.'[15]

Over the next five and a half years, God would lead Hudson, step by step, towards a 'two-fold vision' for China, an extraordinary 'co-mission' that would see the whole of that vast and once forgotten land evangelised. It would be called the China Inland Mission, and Hudson Taylor would be its leader.

Reflection – Dependence

'I will lead the blind by ways they have not known, along unfamiliar paths I will guide them; I will turn the darkness into light before them and make the rough places smooth. These are the things I will do; I will not forsake them.' *(Isaiah 42:16)*

> *'We may make the best plans we can, and then carry them out to the best of our ability... Or, having carefully laid our plans, and determined to carry them through, we may ask God to help us... There is yet another mode of working; to begin with God, to ask His plans, and to offer ourselves to carry out His purposes.'*[16]

Hudson Taylor had an overwhelming, all-consuming passion for evangelisation – proclaiming the gospel to people who had never heard it before. His particular passion was for China and the Chinese. This was a care that God had laid on Hudson's heart since childhood: a care which God nurtured, intensified and realised. The China Inland Mission (CIM) was God's work, Hudson Taylor was simply the channel. But Hudson Taylor had to be willing to be that channel. He had to submit his all to God and God's work, allowing God to lead him, step by step, towards the fulfilment of the vision. God became his all and all, and prayer became the life-blood of the mission. It was a 'two-fold vision' – God and China.

Hudson Taylor had learnt to trust God. But for this extraordinary task to be fulfilled, simply trusting God was not enough. It was complete dependence that God required. Trust and dependence are very closely related, but they are not the same. To trust someone is to believe in them, to have faith in their ability and reliability. To depend on someone is to be totally at their disposal. God needed Hudson Taylor to get to the point where he was completely dependent on Him. He needed to be led by God, step by step: to rest on the power, the wisdom and the strength of the living God. He had to become – metaphorically speaking – blind. God was to be the eyes, the ears, the brain of the CIM; Hudson Taylor was to be simply the channel.

How was this achieved? In the words of Rev J.N. Forman, one of the founders of the Student Volunteer Movement: 'He was a channel – open, clean, and so closely connected with the Fountain of Living Waters that all who came into contact with him were refreshed.'[17]

Hudson Taylor lived close to God. He knew his Bible. He lived a disciplined life. He prayed with strength, belief, intention, humility and passion. He exercised faith abounding. He listened to God, he trusted God and he was obedient to God. His was a 'two-fold vision' and it was God who led the way.

認為 Think

'I trust that in all the days to come, as in the past, we shall recognize our entire dependence upon God and the absolute importance of private and united prayer. How much blessing we owe to our days of prayer, our weekly and daily prayer-meetings, and those of the Councils, will never be known on earth. May God ever shine upon the Mission, and all connected with it at home and abroad, for Christ's sake.'

These were the last words that Hudson Taylor penned as general director of the CIM. Four things particularly stand out: the principle of complete dependence on God; the power of prayer; the reminder that *everything* the mission did was 'for Christ's sake'; and his focus on the future – Hudson Taylor had been called by God to 'go and bear fruit, *fruit that will last*'.

Consider the phrase: 'China's spiritual needs and claims'. Hudson Taylor's 'two-fold vision' was God and China. Is there a person, family, group, tribe, country or cause that replaces the word 'China' in this phrase for you? Is there a 'two-fold vision' that God has lain on your heart? Big or small, if it is a 'two-fold vision', then it comes with 'divine resources'. *Depend* upon it, act upon it. 'God's work, done God's way, will never lack God's supplies.' What a promise!

響應 Respond

'I acted as well as I could, under the circumstances, and those who seek only to know the will of God, and to do it, need not fear missing their providential path. The future is a ravelled maze and my path(s) have ever been made plain one step at a time. I must wait on God and trust in Him, and all will be well.'[18]

In today's world, living one step at a time is a huge challenge which by many would be considered foolish. What about pensions and retirement planning or personal, vocational and financial goals? But if we truly desire to walk with God on 'enchanted ground', to be effective disciples in the cause for Christ, then shouldn't we be more willing to live as Hudson Taylor did – one step at a time?

> *'You do not know what lies before you. I give you one word of advice: Walk with the Lord! Count on Him, enjoy Him. He will not disappoint you.'*

Chapter 7

A SPECIAL AGENCY

(1865–1866)

'God's work, done God's way,
will never lack God's supplies'

'To me it seemed a great calamity that failure of health compelled my relinquishing work for God in China, just when it was more fruitful than ever before; and to leave the little band of Christians in Ningbo, needing much care and teaching, was a great sorrow. Nor was the sorrow lessened when, on reaching England, medical testimony assured me that return to China, at least for years to come, was impossible. Little did I then realize that the long separation from China was a necessary step towards the formation of a work which God would bless as He has blessed the China Inland Mission.'[1]

S

o wrote Hudson Taylor many years later as he reflected on his life and 'God's work'. When he arrived back in England he had no idea of the extent of the co-mission that God had planned for him. The need in China was close to his heart, and the interior a growing concern, but in Hudson's mind this was a work for existing mission organisations to pioneer. If health prevented his return, he would support the work from England. Only as the years passed, and other missions failed to respond to the need, did a view of something greater begin to form in his mind – the need for 'a special agency' to take the gospel to the whole of China. As the need for this special agency grew in his mind, so did the realisation that God meant him to lead it. For several months Hudson Taylor experienced an extreme personal and spiritual battle as he tried to resist the call:

'I had no doubt that, if I prayed for workers in the Name of the Lord Jesus Christ, they would be given me. I had no doubt that, in answer to such prayer, the means for our going forth would be provided, and that doors would be opened before us in unreached parts of the Empire. But I had not then learned to trust God for keeping power and grace for myself, so no wonder that I could not trust Him to keep others who might be prepared to go with me. I feared that in the midst of the dangers, difficulties and trials which would necessarily be connected with such a work, some who were comparatively

inexperienced Christians might break down, and bitterly reproach me for having encouraged them to undertake such an enterprise for which they were unequal.

'*Yet, what was I to do? The feeling of blood-guiltiness became more and more intense. Simply because I refused to ask for them, the labourers did not come forward – did not go out to China – and every day tens of thousands were passing away into Christ-less graves! Perishing China so filled my heart and mind that there was no rest by day, and little sleep by night, till health broke down.*'[2]

Hudson Taylor was learning to trust God for himself, but to trust God for others was a command of quite overwhelming magnitude: 'This was not rebellion, but the soul staggered by a new and great responsibility, before it had grasped afresh the truth that God was greater still.'[3] Hudson did not burden anyone else with his thoughts: 'to no-one could I speak freely', not even his wife, 'I felt I must refrain as long as possible from laying upon her a burden so crushing'.[4] But his state of health was causing

concern, so when in June 1865 George Pearse invited Hudson Taylor to spend a few days with him at Brighton, Hudson gladly accepted.

It was here, on the sands of Brighton beach, that Hudson Taylor received what Dr Martyn Lloyd-Jones described as 'exceptional guidance'.[5] A vision that left the troubled missionary in no doubt. God indeed had a plan for a special agency to take the gospel to China and he, Hudson Taylor, would be its leader:

'On Sunday 25 June 1865, unable to bear the sight of a congregation of a thousand or more Christian people rejoicing in their own security, while millions were perishing for lack of knowledge, I wandered out on the sands alone, in great spiritual agony; and there the Lord conquered my unbelief, and I surrendered myself for this service. I told Him that all responsibility as to issues and consequences must rest with Him, that as His servant, it was mine to obey and follow Him – His, to direct, to care for, and to guide me and those who might labour with me. Need I say that peace at once flowed into my burdened heart? There and then I asked Him for twenty-four fellow-workers, two for each of eleven provinces inland which were without a missionary, and two for Mongolia; and writing the petition on the margin of the Bible I had with me, I returned home with a heart enjoying rest such as it had been a stranger to for months, and with an assurance that God would bless His own work and that I should share in the blessing. I had previously prayed, and asked prayer, that workers might be raised up for the eleven unoccupied provinces, and thrust forth and provided for, but had not surrendered myself to be their leader.'[6]

Hudson Taylor recorded this date in the pocket Bible he had with him in Brighton, with the words: 'Prayed for twenty-four willing, skilful labourers at Brighton June 25, 1865'. Two days later, he responded to this God-given vision and opened an account, at the London and County Bank, in the name of the China Inland Mission. It was with the sum of just £10 and 'all the promises of God'.

Below:
Hudson
Taylor's Bible

Prayed for 24 willing skilful laborers at Brighton, June 25/65.

The address of Bildad.	JOB, XVIII.	Job's belief in the Red—
self against the hypocrite.	B. C. 1520.	4 And be it indeed *that* I have
9 The righteous ° also shall hold on his way, and he that hath clean hands shall be stronger and ʃ stronger.	a Ps. 84.7,11. 1 Pe. 1. 5.	mine ᵇ error remaineth with myself. 5 If indeed ye will magnify *yo* against me, and plead against me
10 But as for you all, do ye return, and come now: for I cannot find *one* wise *man* among you.	b Ga. 6. 5. ʃ add strength.	proach; 6 Know now that God hath over— me, and hath compassed me with
11 My days are past, my purposes ° are broken off, *even* the ᵟ thoughts of my heart.	c Pr. 16. 9. γ or, *violence.* ᵟ *possessions.*	7 Behold, I cry out of γ wrong, b— not heard: I cry aloud, but *ther* judgment.
12 They change the night into day: the light *is* ʃ short because of darkness.	ʃ *near.* η *cried,* or, *called.*	8 He hath fenced up my way cannot pass, and he hath set dark
13 If I wait, the grave *is* mine house: I		

China's spiritual need and claims

There were many defining moments in the life of Hudson Taylor and the China Inland Mission (CIM): his consecration to the service of God as a baby, his conversion, the call to China, the vision on Brighton beach, the opening of the CIM bank account. And then, at midday on 25 October 1865, came another. Hudson Taylor received the first bound copies of *China: Its Spiritual Need and Claims*, a publication which was to have an immensely powerful influence on the Christian world at that time.

Within three weeks the book had to be reprinted. A second edition was published in February 1866, a third in 1868 and a fourth in 1872. In 1884, a large-format fifth edition of 5,000 copies, with a slightly adapted title, *China's Spiritual Need and Claims*, now including maps and illustrations, sold out between June and September prompting a sixth edition in the same year. In 1887, a seventh 'presentation edition' of 10,000 copies was printed, which included a table of Protestant missions in China. An eighth edition followed in 1890. *China's Spiritual Need and Claims* stirred the hearts of many and set in motion God's promised provision for the 'special agency' that Hudson Taylor was now in charge of. The prefatory note of the seventh edition read:

'In the year 1865 I was led to write the pamphlet China's Spiritual Need and Claims, [showing] the urgent necessity there was for some further effort for the evangelization of China. Its circulation was blessed by God, and much interest in China awakened. A number of persons were led to devote themselves to Mission work there; some who joined the China Inland Mission, and some who are members of other Missions, point to that book as having determined their course.'

How did Hudson Taylor achieve this? What was in this pamphlet that so moved so many people? The contents included the biblical justification for mission and the reminder of the 'momentous consequences of our every thought and act'; a reflection on the great antiquity and vast extent of China, its 'spiritual destitution' and overwhelming need; a brief survey on what has been beneficial for China; and accounts of 'impressive experiences' of God's divine interventions on Hudson Taylor's behalf.[7]

There was also an appeal to readers to contemplate the work that still remained among the 'teeming' unevangelised population of China. In 1865 (the year of the first edition of *China's Spiritual Need and Claims*) the following 11 inland provinces were without a missionary presence. (An idea of the size of the province is also given.)

- Gansu – larger than France and Spain together
- Sichuan – nearly as large as Sweden
- Yunnan – as large as Prussia
- Shaanxi – equal in extent to Holland, Saxony, Bavaria, and Wurttemberg
- Shanxi – nearly as large as England and Wales
- Henan – as large as the Austrian States
- Anhui – a little smaller than England
- Jiangxi – twice the size of Portugal
- Hunan – nearly one third larger than Austria
- Guizhou – larger than Belgium, Saxony, Hanover and Bavaria
- Guangxi – nearly equal in extent to England and Wales[8]

Hudson Taylor estimated that there were almost 200 million Chinese in these 11 provinces. Even in the seven coastal provinces where missionaries were already working, if each of the existing missionaries had responsibility for an area equal to eight English cities (an incredible size for just one missionary), he calculated that there would still be 185 million Chinese who would not hear the gospel. This made a total of more than 380 million unevangelised Chinese, not including the outlying dependencies. Hudson was not shy in expressing his concern, nor the challenge, to Christians everywhere:

Above:
Street in Canton

'Whether interesting to us or not, every individual of the millions of China, every inhabitant of these vast regions, must either live or die forever... Every day 33,000, every month 1,000,000 subjects of the Chinese Emperor pass into eternity, without ever having heard the Gospel; and though we may say, "Behold, we knew it not", God will not justify our leaving them to perish on the ground of that excuse.'[9]

'We cannot but believe that the contemplation of these solemn facts has awakened in many the heartfelt prayer, "Lord, what wilt though have me to do, that Thy name may be hallowed? Thy kingdom come, and Thy will be done in China?" It is the prayerful consideration of these facts, and the deepening realisation of China's destitution of all that makes man truly happy, that constrains the writer to lay its claims as a heavy burden upon the hearts of those who have experienced the power of the blood of CHRIST; and to seek, first from the LORD, and then from His people, the men and the means to carry the gospel into every part of this benighted land.'[10]

Hudson Taylor ended his prefatory note to this edition with these words: 'Above all, let us not forget that we all may serve China by prayer to God, without whose aid no other help would avail.' Hudson Taylor left no one out – he called for Christians everywhere to be engaged in the mission for China. It was a heartfelt, spiritual and biblical plea. It was also vital mission intelligence: a thoroughly researched, detailed account of the land, the people and the task. This was no mission based on excess of emotion; this was a God-given task being approached with knowledge, experience, wisdom, intelligence and strategy. And underpinning it all was prayer to a living, all-powerful and faithful God. It was *God's work*, being done in *God's way*, with the assurance – following the 'two-fold vision' and that momentous day in Brighton in June 1865 – that it would not lack *God's supplies*.

In the seventh edition of *China's Spiritual Need and Claims*, published under the title *Formation of the China Inland Mission*, Hudson Taylor wrote these words proving God's faithfulness:

'When Miss Skinner [the last of the five missionaries prayed for] had sailed, the prayer was fully answered which had been first offered to the Lord in China in the year 1859, for five additional labourers for the work in Ningpo [Ningbo] and the province of Cheh-Kiang [Zhejiang]; and we felt in 1865, that in going forward and seeking from the Lord twenty-four more labourers for the interior provinces, we were not entering on a new and untried path of service. The same God who raised up these five workers could raise up others to follow them, and to extend the work into every province of China. We believed that He could – that He would – raise up, "willing, skilful men" for every department of service. All we proposed to do was to lay hold on His faithfulness who called us to this service; and in obedience to His call, and in reliance on His power, to enlarge the sphere of our operations, for the glory of His name who alone doeth wondrous things.'

Recalling his own experience of 'divine resources' and referring to himself, he also wrote: 'For more than twenty-seven years he has proved the faithfulness of God in supplying the pecuniary means for his own temporal wants, and for the need of the work he has been engaged in. He has seen God, in answer to prayer, raising up labourers not a few for this vast mission-field; supplying the means requisite for their outfit, passage, and support; and vouchsafing blessing on the efforts of many of them, both among the native Christians and the heathen Chinese in fourteen out of the eighteen provinces referred to.'[11]

With the formation of the CIM, God began to open the windows of heaven. Hudson Taylor was following God's call and divine resources were being marshalled. A vital form of this came in the support received from 'rope-holders' – significant people who were personally committed to supporting him by giving their particular gifts and resources.[12] Without them, Hudson Taylor would not have been able to fulfil the extraordinary task that God had given him. These 'rope-holders' were God-sent, opportune supplies, from a loving Father to a faithful servant.

'Rope-holders'

William Berger (1815–1899)

William Berger first met Hudson Taylor the evening before his sailing for China. Hudson was a young man of 21, and Berger, a 43-year-old businessman. Berger corresponded with Hudson Taylor while in China and sent the occasional financial gift, which often proved very timely. Back in England, Hudson Taylor and his family were frequent visitors to Saint Hill, the Bergers' country estate in Sussex. This proved a wonderful retreat for the Taylor family, and the friendship between the older, childless couple and the Taylor family a mutual blessing.

Below:
William Berger

Berger was a deeply spiritual man and his business experience made him a perfect confidante and advisor for Hudson Taylor. What really bonded them, though, was their 'growing sense of personal responsibility' towards China and the Chinese. Berger became, in effect, the co-founder and UK Director of the CIM, Hudson Taylor's right-hand man – practically, financially and spiritually. When Hudson Taylor returned to China, it was Berger, helped by his wife Mary, who ran the CIM from England, interviewing and supporting new missionaries. Berger compared the CIM to a tree, a sapling that would 'add slowly to its size and reach as conditions allowed'.

William Berger resigned from his role with the CIM in 1872, mainly due to ill health. He remained a good friend of Hudson Taylor's up to his death in 1899, leaving him a legacy of £1,000. Hudson Taylor donated all of this toward the purchase of 'Berger House', a new headquarters for the CIM in Canada.

Benjamin (1829–1911) and Amelia Broomhall (1835–1918)

Left: Benjamin and Amelia Broomhall with their children

Benjamin had been a great friend of Hudson Taylor from the age of 19 when, as a draper's apprentice, he went to live in Cheapside, Barnsley. Benjamin married Hudson's sister, Amelia, in 1859 while Hudson was in China. Hudson was close to both Benjamin and Amelia and it was his hope that one day they would join him in China. This was never to be, but they were lifelong supporters of Hudson's work – personally and practically. In 1875, Benjamin and Amelia agreed to take over the roles undertaken by William and Mary Berger, a decision which meant moving with their ten children from their Surrey home to the CIM headquarters in Pyrland Road, North London. In 1878, Benjamin was formally appointed the General Secretary to the CIM and his role included the main editorial work for *China's Millions*, extensive correspondence, public relations work, preaching and speaking engagements, and recruiting and supporting new missionaries. Amelia became a house-mother to candidates preparing for China: a strong spiritual and maternal influence.

Benjamin Broomhall preferred to be the man behind the

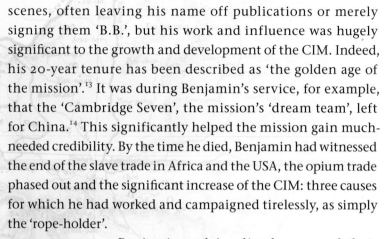

scenes, often leaving his name off publications or merely signing them 'B.B.', but his work and influence was hugely significant to the growth and development of the CIM. Indeed, his 20-year tenure has been described as 'the golden age of the mission'.[13] It was during Benjamin's service, for example, that the 'Cambridge Seven', the mission's 'dream team', left for China.[14] This significantly helped the mission gain much-needed credibility. By the time he died, Benjamin had witnessed the end of the slave trade in Africa and the USA, the opium trade phased out and the significant increase of the CIM: three causes for which he had worked and campaigned tirelessly, as simply the 'rope-holder'.

Below: Book cover showing the 'Cambridge Seven'

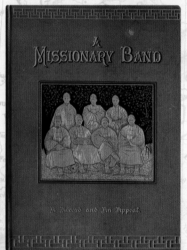

Benjamin and Amelia also opened their home to the Taylor children when Jenny (Hudson Taylor's second wife) needed to return to China to support Hudson on the mission field, increasing their family from ten children to 17! Amelia became mother to them all, prioritising time every day for prayers with them all individually and continuing the 'godly heritage' of her own childhood. Benjamin and Amelia lived to see five of their own children become missionaries in China – four with the CIM (Gertrude, Hudson, Edith and Marshall) and one as an independent missionary (Benjamin junior) – enabling them to fully empathise with both the joys and the heartache felt by parents of candidates leaving for China.

George Muller (1805–1898)

George Muller was a spiritual friend and mentor to Hudson Taylor, as well as a significant financial 'rope-holder'. We read that 'he gave time whenever Mr Taylor visited him to careful consideration of matters connected with the work, his judgement being no less valued than his helpful spirit'.[15] Hudson was particularly influenced by George Muller's approach to mission, prayer and debt: approaches he replicated in his own life and mission.

Alongside the many orphans that George Muller cared and provided for, he also faithfully supported other missions and missionaries, including the CIM. In 1869, he sent cheques to 11 CIM missionaries, and for the next few years his gifts amounted to nearly £2,000 annually. He was now assisting 21 missionaries, who with their 12 wives 'constituted the entire staff of the mission, including Mr and Mrs Taylor'.[16] It is surely an incredible testimony to the faithfulness of God that George Muller – himself a missionary living in complete dependence on God – had sufficient funds to supply such generous 'divine resources' to Hudson Taylor. Incredibly in 1886, when George Muller was 81 years of age, he travelled to China and met with Hudson Taylor in Shanghai.

Above:
George Muller

C.H. Spurgeon (1834–1892)

Hudson Taylor and C.H. Spurgeon first met in 1864 when Hudson and Maria went to hear him preach at the Metropolitan Tabernacle. From that day, the two men enjoyed a life-long friendship and respect for each other. Hudson Taylor even had a portrait of C.H. Spurgeon in an honoured place in his office. Spurgeon financially supported the work of the CIM and directed many missionary candidates to apply to it, saying that 'no other missionary enterprise is so completely to our mind as the China Inland Mission', he stated. In the 1879 edition of *The Sword and the Trowel magazine*, in an article entitled 'Interviews with three of the King's Captains', Spurgeon recalls a visit by Hudson Taylor to his residence in Mentone, France. The talk was almost entirely about China.

Below:
C.H. Spurgeon

Spurgeon's words give a lovely flavour of their conversation, and Hudson's passion for China: 'The word China, China, China is now ringing in our ears in that special, peculiar, musical, forcible, unique way in which Mr Taylor utters it. He could not very readily be made to speak upon any other theme for long together; he would be sure to fly back to China. We believe that he dreams of chop-sticks, mandarins, and poor Chinese.'

Sir Thomas and Lady Catherine Beauchamp and family

Just a week after his visit to Brighton, Hudson Taylor was invited to breakfast by the Dowager Lady Radstock, following his attendance at a small gathering of 'Open Brethren' in Welbeck Street, London. At this breakfast he met Lady Beauchamp of Langley Park, Norfolk. The Beauchamps were 'thoroughly in sympathy with the aims and spirit of their guest' and subsequently arranged for several meetings at their home in Norfolk, to which Hudson Taylor was invited. Sir Thomas and Lady Catherine also desired to support the CIM financially, but their generosity in other directions had left them little to spare for the purpose. After much prayer, they decided to contribute the amount due for the insurance of their many conservatories, trusting God instead for their protection. When storms of 'exceptional violence' hit their neighbourhood later that year, God did not forget. 'Much glass was shattered for miles around, but the conservatories at Langley Park entirely escaped.'[17] God not only supplied the resource, he honoured the means – and the faith – by which it was given.

The Beauchamp's fourth child, Montagu Beauchamp, later became one of the 'Cambridge Seven', giving up a potentially prestigious career for mission work in China. He sailed for China in 1885 and completed many evangelistic journeys,

Above:
Montagu
Beauchamp

some, including one to Australia, in the company of Hudson Taylor. Montagu Beauchamp served the CIM for a total of 30 devoted years.

There were many more 'rope-holders': George Pearse, Rev F.F. Gough, Thomas Barnado, Lord Radstock (son of Lady Radstock mentioned previously), William Fry, Grattan Guinness, and Dixon Hoste, to name just a few. Each had their part to play. Each were a 'divine resource' sent by God to help with Hudson Taylor's extraordinary co-mission, the China Inland Mission.

'To the farthest corners...'

'In June 1865 a thirty-three year old and his wife of twenty-eight proposed to take a score of inexperienced people younger than themselves beyond the treaty ports of China, where the peculiarities of "barbarians" were at least familiar, deep into the interior. All the prejudices, hatreds and physical hazards lay before them. But the antagonism of Satan the "adversary" was most daunting. All of them were agreed in trusting in God alone, not in remote committee, for the necessities of life. And all faced the high risk of losing their lives or health. In the spirit of David Livingstone (himself a missionary in response to Charles Gutzlaff's appeals) – "Can the love of Christ not carry the missionary where the slave trade carries the trader?" – nothing was too much for the just-born China Inland Mission to undertake.'

A strong relationship had been developing at Coborn Street. It had impressed James Meadows on his first day in London. A mutual confidence and affection to which everything else was subordinate, it rode above the annoyances and injuries of day-to-day life. It could reach to the farthest corners of China.

Love was the atmosphere, but obedience was the single secret of its existence. If, once Hudson Taylor knew that God's will for him was to call into being this 'special agency' for China and to accept the onus of all it would entail, he had refused, how much he would have lost. God would have used some other instrument. But he did not. Looking back over his youth, from the day of his submission in Barnsley on December 2nd 1849, through his years of testing at Hull and Soho, to the searing crucible of Shanghai, his constancy stands out. Though he flinched, he stood his ground, doing what he believed to be right. He had cultivated this habit of obedience to what he saw as the will of God from that day at home *when he was seventeen*. Following Jesus he 'learned obedience by the things that he suffered'. Never opting for the easy way out, he chose to obey, whatever the cost. More than anything, this fitted him to be given the great assignment that he became willing, on June 25, 1865, to accept.

> *'In the day of small beginnings he had said, "If I had a thousand lives, China should have them. No! not China, but Christ." Within his lifetime he was to see the "Ningbo five" exceed nine hundred, and within the "open century" that number was to be multiplied fourfold.'*[18]

> *'God's work, done God's way, will never lack God's supplies.'*

Reflection – Love

'For God so loved the world that he gave his one and only Son, that whoever believes in him shall not perish but have eternal life. For God did not send his Son into the world to condemn the world, but to save the world through him.' *(John 3:16–17)*

These verses describe the incredible love that God has for the world; a love so great that He sent His only Son to earth to become human, to die that we might live. Christ suffered the most horrific, painful death on the cross: one of the worst, most terrible forms of execution that can be imposed on the human body. In His short life on earth, Christ was also subject to hate, rejection, torture, temptation, mocking, loneliness and grief. Christ knew what it was to be human. The Bible tells us that in the Garden of Gethsemane He sweated blood at the thought of His impending crucifixion, that three times He begged God to take the cup from Him, yet three times He also said, 'but not my will, but yours'. Such was – and is – Christ's love for us and for the world.

Christ's command 'to go and make disciples of all nations' is an expression of this love. Mission and love are two words that surely go hand in hand. The reason that Hudson Taylor risked his all for China is that God had given him a particular love for China and the Chinese. He loved them with a passion even before he had set foot in China, and it was love that drove him. 'Oh! For eloquence to plead the cause of China; for a pencil dipped in fire to paint the condition of this people', he wrote to his sister Amelia in September 1854. And again, 'Our hearts should be moved with Christ-like compassion, when we think of them scattered abroad as sheep having no shepherd; and our whole souls should cry to the great Lord of the harvest to send forth labourers to seek these lost ones, that they may be saved.'

The Bible commands us to love. To love God and to love our neighbour and even our enemies. The deeper our love for God – Father, Son and Holy Spirit – the greater our capacity for Christlike love for humanity, the ultimate expression of which must surely be sharing the good news of the gospel. Hudson Taylor spent his lifetime focused on the cause for Christ in China. Evangelisation was his main passion: getting the news of the gospel to the whole of China, including the vast, inland provinces. But he also followed Christ's example through acts of practical care and compassion. His was a mission of word and deed, driven – purely and simply – by love for God and love for the Chinese.

認為 Think

> *'What is the object of being apprenticed to a builder but to learn to build? What is the outcome of being joined to a Saviour if we do not learn to save?'*[19]

The Bible's teaching on eternity is clear. There is an eternity with God (heaven) and an eternity without (hell). Our time on earth is limited; our time in eternity is not. That is why Christ's last command was to 'go and make disciples of all nations'. Hudson Taylor felt intensely the need to take the gospel to China, where 'a million a month' were 'dying without God'. He and his missionary colleagues were willing to live anywhere and endure anything because they had 'a hunger for souls'. In an increasingly secular world, is this your driving force? If not, why not reflect on how you can support local and worldwide mission?

響應 Respond

'It is a great blessing when God gives one a hunger for souls. A good many of our early workers had it. We get better people now in some ways, better educated and so on, but it is not often you find that real hunger for souls – people willing to live anywhere and endure anything if only souls may be saved. They were very often humble people. If they were to offer to our Mission now, they might not be accepted – George Duncan, for example! But nothing can take its place, or make up for the lack of it... It is so much more important than any ability.'

If you have been inspired to share your faith with others around you, ask God to provide you with opportunities to do so and the right words to say. Be bold – you might be just the right person in the right place at the right time.

'Let us make earth a little less homelike, and souls more precious. Jesus is coming again, and so soon! Will He find us really obeying His last command?'[20]

Below:

Map of China

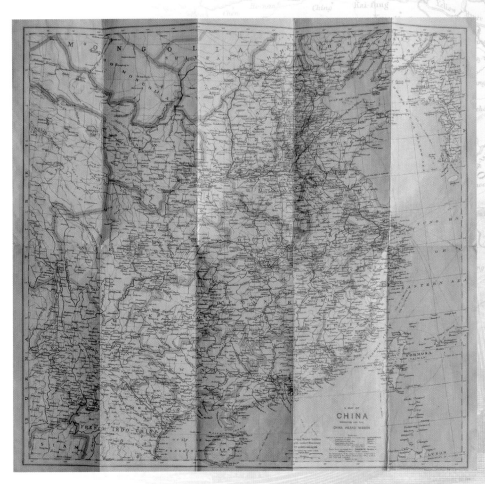

135

Chapter 8

THE EXCHANGED LIFE

(1866–1870)

'Thy will be done'

'Over the dark blue sea, over the trackless flood,
A little band is gone in the service of their God;
The lonely waste of waters they traverse to proclaim,
In the distant land of Sinim, Immanuel's Saving Name.
They have heard from the far-off East the voice of their
brother's blood:
A million a month in China are dying without God...
No help have they but God: alone to their Father's hand
They look for the supply of their wants in a distant land.
The fullness of the world is His – "All power" in earth
and heaven;
They are strong tho' weak, and rich tho' poor, in the
promise He has given.
'Tis enough! They hear the cry, the voice of their
brother's blood:
A million a month in China are dying without God.'[1]

Below:
China Inland
Mission
Occasional Paper

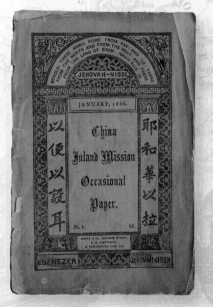

Eleven months elapsed between the vision on Brighton beach and the sailing of the *Lammermuir* in May 1866. These months were 'crowded with fruitful and far-reaching service' and 1866 began with 'fresh assurance, bolder resolutions, and larger enterprises'. The first official publication of the China Inland Mission (CIM) was launched in March under the title *Occasional Papers*, the cost covered by money gifted as a result of prayer.

Alongside loyal friendships, other financial and practical blessings also poured in. The same morning that Hudson Taylor received a gift of £500, he was also offered all the passenger accommodation on board the *Lammermuir*. These simultaneous offers were accepted by the CIM as 'God's ratification of this great venture of faith':

examples of the amazing answers to prayer received from the moment Hudson Taylor submitted to this extraordinary co-mission. Marshall Broomhall describes the attitude of Hudson Taylor and the atmosphere among the supporters of the CIM at that time:

> 'It is interesting to note, at this time, the appearance of a new watchword. The two mottoes Jehovah-Jireh and Ebenezer had been adopted long before in China. Now to these was added a third, Jehovah-Nissi, "The Lord my Banner". It is first seen on the cover of Occasional Papers, and well suits the thought of a forward movement, of an aggressive adventure with the Lord Himself as Captain of the host. It serves too, to show how God was in all his thoughts; it was God who had delivered, it was God who would provide, and it was God who must direct every step of the way.

> 'The secret of Hudson Taylor's strength was God... This was the key of his life. This was the potent truth which made him what he was. All his guiding principles he culled from God's Word. He dared to put Christ's precepts into practice... to turn the other cheek, to seek first God's kingdom, and trust for the rest. Difficulties did not daunt him, but only made him the more resolute.

> '"Every difficulty overcome by faith," he said, "is 'bread' – strength and nourishment – to the child of God. Such the Anakims might have proved to Israel, but Israel failed, and we too often fail from want of faith."'[2]

Hudson Taylor and the missionaries of the CIM were indeed to need 'faith abounding' as they ventured all for Christ. It was just a small band of missionaries that set sail aboard the *Lammermuir* on 26 May 1866 – the Taylor family, one married couple, five single men and, quite incredibly for that time, nine single

women.[3] All were trusting in God as their shield, defender and provider, and in Hudson Taylor as their leader. They had no idea of the testing few years ahead of them.

Above:
The *Lammermuir* band of missionaries

An audacious plan

'All the operations of the Mission are systematic and methodical; and in accordance with, and integral parts of, one general and comprehensive plan for the evangelization of the whole of China.'[4]

Hudson Taylor was a knowledgeable and strategic thinker. He had spent five and a half years in England with the map of China on his study wall and he had studied it in detail. Leading a mission to evangelise the whole of China needed to be approached systematically. Hudson Taylor's policy from the first was: 'to seek an opening in the capital of a province, though it was well known that that was the most difficult place in which to gather a Church. His next step was to open stations in the prefectures, and then in subordinate cities. The chief reasons for this procedure were that the subordinate officials would be afraid and unfriendly if the higher officials had not countenanced the foreigner, and it was anticipated that with Churches in the cities, the villages would be more easily influenced than vice versa.'[5]

Hudson Taylor's strategy, once a station was opened, was to partner with the Chinese. He believed Chinese converts should pastor, with support, the churches the CIM set up in the stations. This freed the CIM missionaries to evangelise in new areas and to set up new stations. Hudson Taylor also believed in the necessity of becoming 'Chinese': adopting Chinese ways and customs 'in everything not sinful'. While this was a pioneering and controversial move among missions and missionaries at that time, it did prove both wise and fruitful.[6]

On arriving in China, the *Lammermuir* party secured a settlement in Hangzhou, the capital of Zhejiang Province. The address was 1 New Lane and it was soon to become an established base for the work of the CIM. By the year 1870, the mission had also acquired 2 New Lane and some additional land on which to build a much-needed chapel. These premises on New Lane housed married couples, families, single men and women, Maria Taylor's vocational school teaching women sewing and reading, Jane (affectionately known as Jennie) Faulding's boys' school, a place for church and related activities, a printing press and a clinic where a day with only 160 patients felt like a holiday!

But Hudson Taylor's vision for the whole of China was ever before his eyes. 'My thoughts are busied,' he wrote in 1867, 'now with the untold need of the unoccupied provinces, now with the neglected districts of this province [Zhejiang], until I am compelled to roll the burden on the Lord, and cry to Him for wisdom to dispose aright of those He may send to help me, and to plead for more Chinese and foreign workers.'

By the end of 1867, just over a year since the

Below:
Plan of No. 1
New Lane

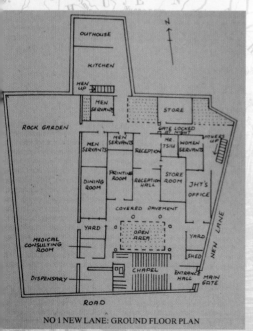

NO 1 NEW LANE: GROUND FLOOR PLAN

party arrived from England, remarkable progress had been made into the interior of Zhejiang Province. The fledgling mission already had eight stations in two provinces, all prefectural cities, with the most remote 24 days' travel apart. Altogether there were now 34 missionaries in the field. But Hudson Taylor was never one to relax his efforts; his eye, driven by a higher cause, 'was ever on the great undone'. The 'immeasurable need' of the immense, unevangelised land of China continued to cry out to him, so that his mind was always fixed on the next step, the next 'advance' in the cause for China and Christ.

Hudson Taylor and the CIM made many advances into the interior between 1866 and 1870. This was a period of immense achievement, but it was also one of immense difficulties. It required the strength, courage, determination and commitment of the men and women who undertook it. Extremes of heat and cold, illness, internal quarrelling and dissention, criticism, riots, danger and death – all threatened to overwhelm the group. In a letter to William Berger in May 1867, Hudson Taylor wrote: 'Burdens such as I have never before sustained, responsibilities such as I had not hitherto incurred, and sorrows compared with which all my past sorrows were light have been part of my experience. But I trust I have, in some feeble measure, learned more of the blessed truth that "Sufficient in His arm alone, And our defence is sure." I have long felt that our mission has a baptism to be baptised with. It may not be past yet. It may be heavier than we can foresee. But if, by grace, we are kept faithful, in the end all will be well.'[7]

Hudson Taylor was right. The next three years were to bring trials much, much 'heavier' than he could ever have foreseen, but with them, grace, strength, even joy in abundance. Hudson was about to be personally tested beyond human strength. However, he was also about to experience a depth of spiritual blessing, which would enable him to say, with confidence: 'No, in all these things we are more than conquerors through him who loved us' (Romans 8:37). The man who had been called by God into the heart of the dragon was about to embark on a very personal journey, which would take him through the deepest valleys of weeping, to the 'eternal springs of God'.

Pengshan was a mountain resort discovered by John McCarthy in 1867. It was in the foothills north of Hangzhou, only six miles away from the mission station. A derelict temple on a forested hill, it had a few habitable rooms which were cared for by a handful of priests. This became the holiday resort of the missionaries at Hangzhou: 'a fairy spot... in the midst of hills and flowers', though with 'tragic memories'.

The garden and the gardener

July 1867 brought with it the expected intense heat: 98 degrees Fahrenheit in the coolest part of 1 New Lane. Many of the household were ill: Hudson Taylor with conjunctivitis; Maria with a debilitating cough and fever; Gracie wasn't eating and was losing weight rapidly; and both Herbert and Frederick were showing signs of serious illness. So Hudson Taylor hired canal and river boats to take them all to the foot of the Pengshan Mountain, where the air was considerably cooler.

'They reached Pengshan on August 5 and on the cool hilltop, living "a gypsy life for a few days" in the derelict temple, three tumbledown sheds and an open pavilion, all quickly improved.'[8]

Unfortunately, this was only a temporary respite. Hudson was soon suffering again, this time with severe pain from suspected renal colic. Young Frederick needed a small operation, which his father had to perform without anaesthesia. Maria had given birth to a baby girl also called Maria but, too weak to feed her, had to rely on a wet nurse for help. But it was Gracie, their firstborn, just eight years old, who was the most seriously ill.

Above: Gracie Taylor

Emily Blatchley arrived at Pengshan to help look after her but by 14 August it was clear to all that she was dying. 'There and then we put her into our Father's hands, pleading with Him to do the best for her and for us,' wrote her broken-hearted father.

Gracie survived just a few more days, her final moments poignantly recorded by A.J. Broomhall: 'Maria sat bowed low over her dying child as all who were well enough stood around the bed singing hymn after hymn, led with a breaking voice by Hudson Taylor. At eight fifty pm on Friday, August 23, her breathing stopped and peaceful beauty spread over her face'.[9] In her father's words, 'the Gardener came and plucked a rose.' Arrangements were swiftly made for Gracie's body to be taken back to Hangzhou for burial. (Had they stayed at Pengshan they would have been forced to have a Chinese funeral.) Little Gracie's body was hidden, among pillows, in a light tin bath, which Hudson Taylor and fellow missionary James Williamson carried downhill, under cover of darkness, to the waiting boat 'Oh that sad, sad, moonlight march,' wrote Hudson Taylor, 'but the Lord sustained us.'

A coffin was carefully and skilfully crafted by Wang Lae-Djun, 'with love that comforted Maria', and a 'little house' built at 1 New Lane (a typical Chinese tomb above ground) in a corner of the rock garden that young Gracie had so enjoyed. When both were ready, all the household, including Maria's 'industrial class of women' and other Chinese friends, gathered for a simple service in the garden, and the 'little house' was sealed. A pencilled note by Maria described the occasion, ending with the words:

'Renew my will from day to day
Blend it with Thine, and take away
All that now makes it hard to say
Thy will be done.'

Words cannot properly convey the suffering of Hudson and Maria at this time. Grief was no less raw, no less real for them than for any other parent grieving the loss of a child. But faith sustained them. A fellow missionary observed: 'It is impossible to separate even in thought the husband and wife at the time. They were sustained and helped to glorify God and be an example to those around of submission and joyful acquiescence in the will of God... There was no desire to take back or keep that which had so fully been given to God.'[10]

Two letters, one written at the bedside of his dying daughter, the other just a few weeks later, reveal something of the heart and mind of the man who was both a faithful servant of the living God and a loving father:

To William Berger, 15 August 1867:

'It was no vain nor unintelligent act when, knowing this land, its people, and climate, I laid my wife and children, with myself, on the altar for this service. And He Whom so unworthily, with much of weakness and failure, yet in simplicity and godly sincerity, we are and have been seeking to serve, and not without some measure of success – He has not left us now.'

And to his mother, September 1867:

*'Our dear little Gracie! How we miss her sweet voice in the morning...
as I take the walks I used to take with her tripping at my side, the
thought comes anew like a throb of agony, "Is it possible that I shall
never more feel the pressure of that little hand, never more hear the
sweet prattle of those dear lips, never more see the sparkle of those
bright eyes?" And yet she is not lost. I would not have her back again.
I am thankful she was taken, rather than any of the others, though
she was the sunshine of our lives... But she is far holier, far happier
than she could ever have been here... Pray for us. At times I am
almost overwhelmed with the internal and external trials connected
with our work. But he has said, "I will never leave thee nor forsake
thee", and "My strength is made perfect in weakness." So be it.'*

Hudson Taylor's 'Personal Pentecost'

It was on 4 September 1869 that Hudson Taylor experienced what
has been described as 'his own personal Pentecost'.[11] From the
beginning of that year he had been deeply dissatisfied with his
spiritual condition and was almost constantly oppressed by an
overwhelming sense of failure: 'I never knew how bad a heart I
had... Often I am tempted to think that one so full of sin cannot
be a child of God at all.' He was like the pilgrim Christian, trapped
in Doubting Castle, imprisoned by Giant Despair: 'Is there no
rescue? Must it be thus to end? I hated myself; I hated my sin; and
yet I gained no strength against it. Hope almost died out.'[12]

His intense grief from the death of his beloved Gracie and the
huge burden of leadership of the mission were highly likely to
have contributed to his current state of mind, but also significant
was his personal reading, and the prominence of the 'Holiness'
movement in England at that time. This movement told of the
potential of a spiritual life on a higher plane, a life revitalised by
the presence of the Holy Spirit. According to Marshall Broomhall,
the 'Spirit of God' was moving upon the hearts of His people in

England and on the mission field in China, causing them to enter into 'a new enjoyment of fullness of life in Christ'.[13]

In the same letter to his sister Amelia, autumn 1869, Hudson wrote: 'My mind has been greatly exercised for six or eight months past, feeling the need personally, and for our Mission, of more holiness, life, power in our souls. But personal need stood first and was the greatest... Each day brought its register of sin and failure, of lack of power. To will was indeed present with me, but how to perform I found not.'

The 'light' came through a letter he received from a fellow-worker, John McCarthy, who had been reading a book from Hudson's own library entitled *Christ Is All*. The following lines were a special help to the struggling pilgrim: 'How then to have our faith increased? Only by thinking of all that Jesus *is,* and all he is *for us.* His life, His death, His work, He Himself as revealed to us in the Word, to be the subject of our constant thoughts. Not a striving to have faith, or to increase our faith, but a looking off to the Faithful One, seems all we need; a resting in the Loved One entirely, for time and eternity. It does not appear to me as anything new, only formerly misapprehended.'[14]

Above:
John McCarthy

As Hudson read the letter, the light was 'to his thirsty soul as living water from the Eternal Springs of God'. He described the change that came over him in the same letter to his sister: 'I looked to Jesus and saw (and when I saw, oh, how the joy flowed!) that he had said "will never leave you". "Ah, *there* is rest," I thought. "I have striven in vain to rest in Him. I'll strive no more. For has *He* not promised to abide with me – never to leave me, never to fail me?" And, dearies, *He never will.*'[15]

Hudson continued to describe to his sister the deep sense of spiritual joy, peace, and power that was now flowing through him:

'But this was not all He showed me, nor one half... The sweetest part, if one may speak of one part being sweeter than another, is the rest

As I thought of the Vine and the branches, what light the blessed Spirit poured direct into my soul! How great seemed my mistake in having wished to get the sap, the fullness out of Him. I saw not only that Jesus would never leave me, but that I was a member of His body, of His flesh and of His bones. The vine now I see is not the root merely, but all—root, stem, branches, twigs, leaves, flowers, fruit: and Jesus is not only that: He is soil and sunshine, air and showers, and ten thousand times more than we have ever dreamed, wished for, or needed. Oh, the joy of seeing this truth! I do pray that the eyes of your understanding may be enlightened that you may know and enjoy the riches freely given us in Christ.

Oh, my dear sister, it is a wonderful thing to be really one with a risen and exalted Saviour; to be a member of Christ! Think what it involves. Can Christ be rich and I poor? Can your right hand be rich and the left poor? or your head be well fed while your body starves? Again, think of its bearing on prayer. Could a bank clerk say to a customer, "It was only your hand wrote that cheque, not you," or "I cannot pay this sum to your hand, but only to yourself"? No more can your prayers, or mine, be discredited *if offered in the Name of Jesus* (i.e. not in our own name, or for the sake of Jesus merely, but on the ground that we are His, His members) so long as we keep within the extent of Christ's credit—a tolerably wide limit! If we ask anything unscriptural or not in accordance with the will of God, Christ Himself could not do that: but "If we ask anything according to His will He heareth us, and . . . we know that we have the petitions that we desire of Him."

The sweetest part, if one may speak of one part being sweeter than another, is the rest which full identification with Christ brings. I am no longer anxious about anything, as I realize this; for He, I know, is able to carry out *His will*, and His will is mine. It makes no matter where He places me, or how. That is rather for Him to consider than for me: for in the easiest positions He must give me His grace, and in the most difficult His grace is sufficient. It little matters to my servant whether I send him to buy a few cash worth of things or the most expensive article. In either case he looks to me for the money, and brings me his purchases. So, if God place me in great perplexity, must He not give me much guidance; in positions of great difficulty, much grace; in circumstances of great pressure and trial, much strength? No fear that His resources will be unequal to the emergency! And His resources are mine, for He is mine, and is with me and dwells in me. All this springs from the believer's oneness with Christ, and since Christ has thus dwelt in my heart by faith, how happy I have been! I wish I could tell you instead of writing about it.

Your own affectionate brother,
J. HUDSON TAYLOR.

(The complete letter, of which the foregoing is a part, will be found in the second volume of Hudson Taylor's life, entitled *Hudson Taylor and the China Inland Mission*.)

Copies of this leaflet, for distribution, can be had on application to the China Inland Mission, Newington Green, London, N.16, at 3s. 0d. per dozen post free.

which full identification with Christ brings. I am no longer anxious about anything, as I realize this; for He, I know, is able to carry out His Will, and His Will is mine... I feel and know that old things have passed away. I am as capable of sinning as ever, but Christ is realized as present as never before... And further – walking more in the light, my conscience has been more tender; sin has been instantly seen, confessed, pardoned; and peace and joy (with humility) instantly restored... Faith, I now see, is "the substance of things hoped for", and not mere shadow. It is not less than sight, but more. Sight only shows the outward form of things; faith gives the substance. You can rest on substance, feed on substance. Christ dwelling in the heart by faith (i.e. His Word of Promise credited) is power indeed, is life indeed.'

Above: Hudson Taylor's letter to his sister printed in *The Exchanged Life* booklet

Hudson's 'personal Pentecost' was perhaps his most important spiritual experience after his conversion. It led to 'the exchanged life', a life that *rested* in Christ alone. Many years previously he had offered up his life in service to his Lord and Master, but this was something more, something far deeper, more powerful. He had 'exchanged' his life with Christ. This gave him a sense of joy, assurance, peace, power and strength such as he had never known before.

'God's clocks keep good time,' he once said;[16] and never more so than in 1869. Hudson Taylor's 'personal Pentecost' was indeed timely provision from a loving heavenly Father to a human one. The following year Hudson was to experience yet another 'Valley of Weeping', this time a much deeper, darker, lonelier valley. But the spiritually renewed pilgrim had exchanged his life with Christ and could now say, with complete conviction, of *any* situation, 'If satisfied with His will and way, *there is rest.*'[17]

Overwhelming sorrows

1870 was to be a year filled with, humanly speaking, overwhelming sorrows and anxieties. At the start of the year Hudson and Maria decided they should send the four eldest children – Herbert, Frederick, Samuel and Maria – to England to escape the great heat of the approaching summer. This was

Below: Hudson and Maria Taylor with their children Gracie, Howard, Samuel and Herbert

planned for the end of March, and the parting loomed like a very 'dark cloud' over the devoted parents. But just a few weeks before departure, young Samuel, only five years old, suddenly became sick and died. It was with even heavier hearts, therefore, that Hudson and Maria waved farewell to the remaining three at the close of March. Only little Charles (born in November 1868) stayed with them.

In June, the Tianjin Massacre took place, necessitating the removal of some missionary workers from their stations to the increasingly crowded mission premises in Zhenjiang. 'One difficulty follows another very fast,' Hudson

Taylor wrote from here to the team in Hangzhou at the end of June. On 5 July, Maria Taylor was seized with cholera two days before giving birth to their fifth son, Noel. Maria was too weak to nurse her new baby and just 13 days later little Noel breathed his last. In a letter home to Barnsley, Hudson Taylor wrote of the countenance of his wife at this time: 'Though excessively prostrate in body, the deep peace of soul, the realisation of the Lord's own presence, and the joy in His holy will with which she was filled, and in which I was permitted to share, I can find no words to describe.'

Above: Emily Blatchley with Herbert, Frederick and Maria

Maria Taylor lived just long enough to choose the hymns for her baby's funeral and to receive a much-awaited letter from Mary Berger, lovingly written with news that the Taylor children had arrived safely in England. At 9am on Saturday 23 July, Maria Taylor passed peacefully into the everlasting arms of her Saviour. The final moments of the devoted wife, mother and child of God recorded by Hudson Taylor convey, very movingly, the depth of love Hudson and Maria shared, both for each other and for God.

'My precious wife thought of my being left alone at a time of so much trial, and with no companion like herself, with whom I had been wont to bring every difficulty to the Throne of Grace.

"I am so sorry," she said, and paused as if half correcting herself for the feeling.

"You are not sorry to go to be with Jesus?"

*Never shall I forget that look with which she answered, "Oh, no!
It is not that. You know, darling, that for ten years past there has
not been a cloud between me and my Saviour. I cannot be sorry to
go to Him; but it does grieve me to leave you alone at such a time.
Yet... He will be with you and meet all your need."*[18]

'I never witnessed such a scene,' wrote Mrs Duncan, a few
days later. 'As dear Mrs Taylor was breathing her last, Mr Taylor
knelt down – his heart so full – and committed her to the Lord;
thanking Him for having given her, and for the twelve and a half
years of happiness they had had together; thanking Him, too, for
taking her to His own blessed presence, and solemnly dedicating
Himself anew to His service.'

Hudson Taylor was broken-hearted: Herbert, Frederick and
Maria were far away in England, his beautiful new-born son had
lived just a few short days and now his beloved wife had gone to
be with the Lord. This was grief and circumstance greater than
any human spirit surely could endure; the deepest, darkest,
loneliest valley of weeping. But Hudson had learnt to drink from
the 'eternal springs of God'. Even amidst overwhelming sorrows,
there was rest. 'I scarcely knew whether she or I was the more
blessed, so real, so constant, so satisfying was His presence, so
deep my delight in the consciousness that His will was being
done, and that that Will, which was utterly crushing me, was
good, and wise, and best."[19]

'What a promise!' Hudson Taylor wrote some years later,
speaking of his revelations in the midst of his suffering. "'*Shall
never thirst.*" To know that "shall" means shall; that "never"
means never; that "thirst" means any unsatisfied need, may
be one of the greatest revelations God ever made to our souls.
Let us not, however,' he adds, 'change the Saviour's words.
Note carefully He does not say, Whosoever has drunk, but
"drinketh". He speaks not of one draught, but of the continuous
habit of the soul.'[20]

'Because God is God'

Hudson Taylor had learnt, through immense personal suffering, to release *all* claims on earthly life. And not just his, but those of his wife and children also – they were all strangers in a strange land. Eternity was their focus, their strength, their hope. The presence of God was now a living, constant reality; peace, strength, comfort, and power flowed through him from the knowledge that God's will was 'good, and wise, and best'. The way of duty was still the way of safety. From now on Hudson Taylor would be in an 'invulnerable position'.

> *'We conclude, therefore, that Job was not mistaken, and that we shall not be mistaken if we follow his example, in accepting all God's providential dealings as from Himself. We may be sure that they will issue in ultimate blessing; because God is God, and therefore, "all things work together for good to them that love Him."*[21]

By faith Hudson Taylor stood, and by faith he would advance.

Reflection – God's sovereignty

'And we know that in all things God works for the good of those who love him, who have been called according to his purpose.' *(Romans 8:28)*

Reading the moving accounts of the deaths of Hudson Taylor's precious daughter Gracie, his young son Samuel, his new-born son Noel, and his beloved wife Maria, it is hard to imagine such suffering all in the space of just three years. Hudson Taylor was a devoted husband and father; Maria was his beloved wife, his children his joy and delight. Now Hudson found himself almost entirely alone in China. His three eldest children had sailed for England just months before. Only little Charles remained.

There is no doubt that Hudson Taylor grieved as intensely as anyone would at such a time. His letters are testament to this. But they are also testament to his unswerving faith in a loving, faithful and *sovereign* God. In a letter to his mother, a few days before losing baby Noel, he wrote:

'I find increasing comfort in the thought that all things are really in our Father's hand and under His governance. He cannot but do what is best. "God nothing does nor suffers to be done, But we would do the same, could we but see through all events of things as well as He."'[22]

In a letter to William Berger, just days after the death of Maria, he wrote:

'And now, dear brother, what shall I say of the Lord's dealings with me and mine? I know not! My heart is overwhelmed with gratitude and praise. My eyes flow with tears of mingled joy and sorrow. When I think of my loss, my heart – nigh to breaking – rises in thankfulness to Him Who has spared her such sorrow and made her so unspeakably happy. My tears are more tears of joy than of grief. But most of all I joy in God through our Lord Jesus Christ – in His works, His ways, His providence, in Himself. He is giving me to prove (to know by trial) "What is that good and acceptable and perfect will of God." I do rejoice in that will. It is acceptable to me; it is perfect; it is love in action.'[23]

And then on 4 August, once again to his mother, Hudson wrote:

'I have just been reading over my last letter to you, and my views are not changed, though chastened and deepened. From my inmost soul I delight in the knowledge that God does or deliberately permits all things, and causes all things to work together for good to those who love Him.'[24]

It is easy to trust God's will as perfect when life is going well; so much harder at times of difficulty and trial. But God promises that He will work *all things* for good. This is why Hudson Taylor's response to adversity is such an important lesson – he recognised that God's will was perfect in *every* situation. Even amidst the most incredible grief, Hudson Taylor was able to enjoy strength, comfort, hope, rest – even joy.

認為 Think

'The secret of it all was Hudson Taylor's simple, childlike unshakable faith in God. He is simply inconceivable apart from his faith in the Word, and character of God. There is no other explanation of the man. What he was, and what he did, sprang from no other root, had no other origin. God's character was his only confidence; God's Word was the sole foundation for his feet. These were the eternal truths which inspired him; these were the secret of his strength, the reason and justification of his enterprise, the ground of his convictions, the fount of his joy, and the rock on which he built. If there is one Scripture, more than another, inseparably associated with his name, it is: "Have faith in God"... "Oh for the clear accent, the ringing, joyous note of apostolic assurance!" wrote one who is now beyond the veil. "We want a faith not loud, but deep; a faith not born of sentiment and human sympathy, but that comes from the vision of the Living God." It was this that Hudson Taylor possessed. It was this that he enjoyed. He believed God.'[25]

So wrote Marshall Broomhall in the opening chapter to his book *The Man Who Believed God*. Hudson Taylor believed in a faithful, loving, living and *sovereign* God, a God whose will – even in the most difficult and challenging of circumstances – was 'good, and wise, and best'. This was how Hudson Taylor was enabled to experience 'the peace of God, which transcends all understanding' (Philippians 4:7), even at a time of intense personal tragedy. Such faith is a powerful demonstration of the Christian hope, and of the freedom found in Christ alone.

響應 Respond

'I feel like a little child... But with the weakness of a child I have the rest of a child. I know my Father reigns: this meets questions of every kind. I have heard today that war has broken out in Europe, between France and Prussia; that it is rumoured that England joins the former and Russia the latter. If so, fearful doings may be expected; but, "the Lord reigneth".'[26]

Hudson Taylor was writing just days after losing his wife and child. He was experiencing incredible grief and intense loneliness, and now there was the threat of war. But in all this, Hudson Taylor was able to experience 'the rest of a child'. Why? Because he knew that *everything* was within the will of an all-powerful and sovereign God; that God does work *all things* for good. In our very unsettled and often troubled world, can you say that you have *the rest of a child*, that complete and unswerving trust – even at the worst of times – in the wisdom, the power and the love of God?

'All things work together for good'

Chapter 9

ALWAYS ADVANCING

(1871–1887)

*'Nor is God's work ever
intended to be stationary,
but always advancing.'*[1]

Hudson Taylor sailed for England in the autumn of 1871. His five years in China had been rich in activity and blessing, but they had also been years of severe trial and hardship. Alongside the deaths of three of his children, Gracie, Samuel and Noel, and his beloved wife Maria, Hudson had been severely tried in a host of other ways: 'personal sickness, by baneful consequences of the Tianjin massacre, by strenuous efforts of the Chinese government to restrict missionary liberty, by shortness of funds... and by Mr Berger's request to be relieved of responsibility for the Home Department of the Mission.'[2] The 'responsibility' of the mission ultimately rested with God, but Hudson Taylor still felt it deeply, and with the death of Maria, he now had no soulmate on earth with whom to share it.

An insight into how he was feeling at this time is found in the following few lines from a letter to his mother, written on the voyage home: 'My life work *for* China is far from accomplished, though I am not sure that my work *in* China may not be largely done. One year has been clean lost, and I cannot really and effectively resume it alone.' Hudson Taylor was not yet 40 years of age. The grief and loneliness, combined with the responsibilities of the mission, were overwhelming. It is no wonder that he questioned his role and even whether he would return to China.

But Hudson did return to China. God's work for him in that vast land was far from over. In fact, in many ways it had hardly begun. From 1871–1887 much was to happen and many important advances were to be made in the evangelisation of China.

The first important event was the marriage of Hudson Taylor and Jane (Jennie) Faulding, which took place on 28 November 1871 at Regent's Park Chapel, London. Jennie had been a faithful supporter of the China Inland Mission almost from its inception, attending regular prayer meetings at the Taylors' home. In 1865 she had graduated from the Home and Colonial Training College with Emily Blatchley, both girls joining the *Lammermuir* party that sailed for China in May 1866. Jennie had proved herself a devoted and industrious missionary, adopting Chinese dress and throwing herself into the work, particularly among Chinese women. She had felt the death of Maria Taylor very keenly, for Maria had been a great friend and mentor to her from the earliest days of the mission in London.

Above:
Hudson and
Jennie Taylor

It was perhaps not unsurprising then, that just a little more than a year after the death of Maria, Hudson Taylor and Jennie Faulding should find themselves drawn to each other in a bond of mutual love, respect and purpose. Hudson proposed on the voyage home, and after some persuasion, Jennie's parents granted the couple their blessing. A home was established in 6 Pyrland Road, London, a home which also was to serve as the UK mission headquarters on the retirement of William Berger in 1872. Hudson and Jennie were blessed with two children of their own during these years: Ernest Hamilton Taylor, born January 1875, and Amy Taylor, born April 1876. (Earlier in April 1873 twins had been born, an unnamed boy and girl, but did not survive.) They also adopted Mary Jane Bowyer Duncan, the orphan child of a missionary couple in 1877. Hudson and Jennie enjoyed a happy marriage, a deeply spiritual union combined with a shared passion for God and China, but overshadowed by long months, even years, of separation from each other and from their children.

There were further personal challenges for the couple. In May 1874, Hudson Taylor had a serious fall while on a visit to Wuchang with a fellow missionary. With Emily Blatchley, the guardian of his children, seriously ill in England, Hudson was keen to return to be with her and his children. But when he and Jennie arrived in England in October 1874, Emily had already died and Hudson, due to his fall, was faced with the possibility of never being able to walk again. He spent months confined to bed, at times even unable to write. Thankfully, by August the following year, Hudson was restored to health and he was able to join his children on holiday in Guernsey. Ill health, though, was to plague Hudson Taylor on many occasions, at times severely limiting the work he would have liked to do. But illness enabled him to focus and advance in other ways, as he observed to his wife in November 1876: 'The weakness that prevents overwork may be the greatest blessing to me.'

Above: 6 Pyrland Road, London

Politically there were challenges too. In February 1875, a British official, Augustus Raymond Margary, and his entire staff were murdered during an exploration of overland trade routes between British India and China. This led to a diplomatic crisis between Britain and China. Tensions between the Chinese and foreign residents, including missionaries, intensified, and for a period of two years 'advances' in evangelism were limited. The crisis was resolved in September 1876 when the Chefoo Convention was signed and tensions were eased. In the providence of God and in answer to much prayer, it also granted extraterritorial privileges for British subjects in China, and further treaty ports were opened as part of a new trade agreement. The significance of this to the mission, stated Marshall Broomhall, 'may be gathered from the fact that during the next eighteen months its pioneers travelled more than thirty thousand miles throughout the Empire making known the Gospel'.[3] So it was that, time after time, trials turned into wonderful 'advances', and sufferings into 'showers of blessing'.

'Out of weakness made strong'

Hudson Taylor's writing during this period is littered with reflections on the synergy between trial and blessing. He wrote as one who knew this from personal experience, but also as one with a depth of faith that expected nothing less. Indeed, for Hudson Taylor, trials were counted 'more precious than gold',[4] and personally viewed as an intrinsic part of his role as leader of the mission: 'It is a specially sweet part of God's dealings with His messengers, that He always gives us the message for ourselves first... He does not send us out with sealed despatches.'[5] Though often painful beyond measure, he accepted them with the wisdom of one who perceives the difficult times as all part of God's ultimate plan – a plan that is 'good, and wise, and best'. Hudson's reflections on trials were full of encouragement and comfort:

'Difficulties afford a platform upon which He can show Himself.'[6]

'I believe that God has enabled me to do more for China during this long illness than I might have done had I been well.'[7]

'There must be a good deal more effected by pain than we know of at present. It seems essentially connected with fruitfulness, natural and spiritual.'[8]

'There is trial on every hand... In the midst of it all God is revealing Himself. The work is wonderfully advancing, and those who will have it are getting showers of blessing.'[9]

It was Hudson Taylor's practice of reflecting on the providence of God, trusting in the faithfulness of God, praying to a living God, and walking in God's will one step at a time that enabled him to find in God 'an unchanging source of strength and joy',[10] even during the most difficult of circumstances. A beautiful and challenging passage from an article of his entitled *Blessed Adversity* encapsulates his response to suffering:

'The believer does not need to wait until he sees the reason of God's afflictive dealings with him ere he is satisfied; he knows that all things work together for good to them that love God; that all God's dealings are those of a loving Father, who only permits that which for the time being is grievous in order to accomplish results that cannot be achieved in any less painful way. The wise and trustful child of God rejoices in tribulation... Our Heavenly Father delights to trust a trustworthy child with a trial in which he can bring glory, and through which he will receive permanent enlargement of heart and blessing for himself and others.'[11]

'It was this determination to see God only in every trial, and not to look at second causes, that was his strength', wrote Marshall Broomhall. 'It was his faith in God over all, through all, and in all, that gave him the victory.' It is easy to read such words, but they fundamentally affect the life of the person who believes them – and Hudson Taylor did believe them. It was the audacity of faith in tribulation. Trials and opposition only spurred him to fresh effort to advance God's kingdom. For Hudson, the best defence was to advance, and from the beginning he had laid plans for such advance. In his own words: 'All the operations of the Mission are systematic and methodical; and in accordance with, and integral parts of, one general and comprehensive plan for *the evangelization of the whole of China*.'[12]

Wonderful advances

Above:
Chinese
missionaries

Inspirational men and women of the CIM undertook dangerous journeys for the purpose of spreading the gospel to remote areas of China and Tibet, resulting in wonderful advances for the cause of Christ. Statistics produced by CIM reviewing the first two decades of the mission, provide a general view of progress.[13] A brief summary of the first decade (1865–1875) reveal that CIM had established 28 churches and 56 stations and out-stations with the help of 36 missionaries and 76 Chinese colleagues.

The following decade (1875–1885), CIM reach had extended to a further nine inland provinces. There were now 45 churches and 141 stations and out-stations underpinned by 137 missionaries and 106 Chinese workers. On top of this, 16 schools were founded and 1,764 Chinese people had been baptised into the Christian faith.[14]

Home Council

With the resignation of William Berger as director of the mission at home, Hudson Taylor recognised the need for a better management structure in England. On 6 August 1872, the Home Council was formally established, meeting for the first time that October. Based in London, initially at 6 Pyrland Road, the members were: Richard Hill, Henry Soltau (Hon. Secretary), John Challice (Hon. Treasurer), George Soltau (candidate training), William Hall, Theodore Howard, Joseph Weatherly, and Emily Blatchley (editor of the *Occasional Paper*). In 1878,

Benjamin Broomhall was appointed General Secretary of the CIM, a role he held for 20 years – a period referred to as 'the golden age of the Mission'.

Headquarters in Shanghai

The first CIM headquarters was established in November 1873 in the American settlement. Five small local shops were acquired and adapted so that they were all connected with a long upstairs passage. The first occupants to move in the following month were Edward and Annie Fishe.

In 1886, a piece of land on the Wusong Road went up for sale. Archibald Orr-Ewing, recently arrived from England and in possession of a large estate, offered to fund the entire cost of building the new headquarters. Construction began in April 1887 and by February 1890 it was ready for use. It became the headquarters for the CIM for the following 40 years.

Above: Original headquarters of the China Inland Mission in Shanghai

Appeal for workers: 'Eighteen', 'Seventy', 'One Hundred'

Three formal appeals for workers were made: the first in 1875 when Hudson Taylor was confined to bed. He appealed to God for 18 workers to cover the nine unreached inland provinces. God gave him 24, including six missionaries already in China who applied to join the CIM.

The second appeal was in 1881: Hudson Taylor appealed to God for 70 new workers to join within the next three years. By 1884, 76 new members had joined the CIM, including the two eldest children of Benjamin and Amelia Broomhall (Gertrude and Hudson) and four of the 'Cambridge Seven' (Hoste, Smith,

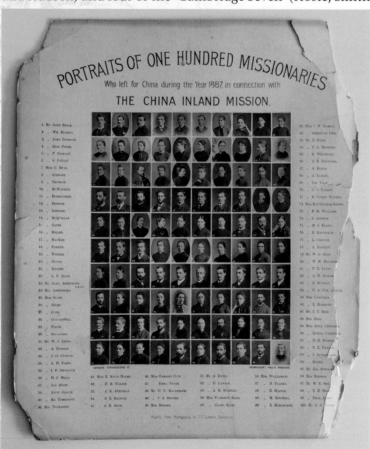

Right:
The 'One Hundred' missionaries

Cassels and Studd). Of the year 1884, Howard and Geraldine Taylor wrote: 'It was the last of the three years in which the Seventy were to be given, according to the faith that had received them from the Lord; and given they were in royal fashion – most of the large party that sailed toward the end of October being over and above the number. Forty-six in all were sent out during the twelve months; and it was not only the number but the calibre of the workers that was remarkable. Often must Mr Taylor have been reminded of the prayer going up from many hearts that the Seventy might be *God-sends* as well as God-sent to China.'[16]

A letter written by John Stevenson to Jennie Taylor, dated 16 September 1886, contained the first suggestion of the 'one hundred fresh labourers'. A few weeks later, the following words were cabled to London: 'Praying for a hundred new missionaries in 1887'. By the close of 1887, 102 missionaries had sailed for China.

Below:

Early edition of *China's Millions*

China's Millions

A new monthly publication replaced the *Occasional Paper*, which was by now unfit for purpose, called *China's Millions*. It was first issued in July 1875 and was rightly described as 'a great undertaking' and 'an innovation': 'Its up-to-date articles and pictures, when Burma was occupying a good deal of public attention; its Chinese stories brightly translated for young people, and full-page texts with floral designs for children to colour on Sundays; its news of pioneer

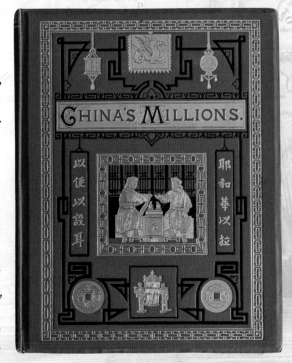

journeys, and of conversions and progress in the older stations; and above all its spiritually helpful articles from Mr Taylor's pen came to be looked for by friends old and new.'[17] Like *China's Spiritual Need and Claims*, this publication proved enormously fruitful in raising new workers, new friends and fresh supplies for the CIM.

General Missionary Conference: Shanghai, 10–24 May 1877

During a conference encompassing all mission organisations in China, Hudson Taylor presented a paper entitled *Itineration Far and Near, as an Evangelising Agency*, which 'secured the deepest interest of his audience'. Howard and Geraldine Taylor recorded the impact of this conference:

> 'From Dr John's opening address with its searching, powerful appeal for a life in the Holy Spirit, to the call of the united conference "to the Mission Boards, Colleges and Churches of the World" for men and women to meet the great opportunity, all was cause for thanksgiving – "a gathering fraught with blessing to the people of China," as Mr Taylor wrote, "the most important step China missions have yet taken." The parting, after two weeks of fellowship was "like the breaking-up of a family never more to meet on earth." No discordant note remained. Even the Chinese dress of Mr Taylor and his fellow-workers had ceased to offend, and the forward movement they represented had passed into the confidence and prayerful sympathy of most if not all present.'[18]

Chefoo school

The need for a school and a convalescent home for sick missionaries was inspired by a visit to Chefoo (Yantai) by Hudson Taylor in 1879, himself needing significant rest. He

invited C.H. Judd (a fellow missionary) and his family to join him, and together they prayed for God's direction for such a venture. A plot of neighbouring farm land had providentially become available at a very reasonable price, which the CIM purchased. 'I never knew a piece of business settled so easily', recalled Mr Judd. To save money, Hudson Taylor suggested they quarried their own stone, employing local men for the task. Hudson was 'his own architect', even sourcing oak, pine and teak from two ships wrecked in the bay. Cabin fittings from one of them were also utilised to great effect, including doors, locks, cupboards and 'a splendid sideboard'. Judd's account of the build demonstrates the ingenuity of Hudson Taylor and his fellow workers:

Above:
Chefoo

Below:
C.H. Judd

> 'I do not say that the house was well built, but it was wonderfully good considering our lack of experience. There were five rooms upstairs and about as many down, with out-house and lean-to rooms besides. It was marvellously cheap; and the Europeans in the Settlement were amazed at the rapidity with which it was put up. They could hardly believe their eyes when they saw it finished!'[19]

Chefoo School opened in January 1881 with only three students. By 1882, 14 students had enrolled. By 1886, it had over 100 students on roll, and was divided into three sections: Boys, Girls and Preparatory. With a rigorous curriculum based on the British system, it was described as 'the best English-speaking school east of the Suez'.[20]

Dr Harold Schofield spent only three years in China, dying in 1883 from typhus. He had prayed earnestly in the preceding six months for the best quality workers to be sent to China. On the day he died, 1 August 1883, Hudson Taylor received a letter from the first of the Cambridge Seven, Dixon Hoste: the man who would one day take over from Hudson Taylor as director of CIM.

The 'Cambridge Seven'

The 'Cambridge Seven' was the answer to Dr Harold Schofield's dying prayer.

The mission's 'dream team' left for China in February 1885 and was comprised of: Dixon E. Hoste, C.T. Studd, Stanley P. Smith, Montagu Beauchamp, William Cassels, Cecil Polhill-Turner and Arthur Polhill-Turner. All had connections with Cambridge and distinguished social backgrounds, including merchants, athletes and the royal army. Each had surrendered personal ambitions and bright futures, some even significant inheritances, to give all for God and the cause for Christ in China. Of the 'Cambridge Seven', Eugene Stock (editorial secretary of the Church Missionary Society), commented:

> *'The influence of such a band of men going to China was irresistible. No such event had occurred before; and no event of the century had done so much to arouse the minds of Christian men to the tremendous claims of the Field, and the nobility of the missionary vocation.'*[21]

Pastor Hsi

Pastor Hsi had been an opium addict and Confucian scholar before being converted through the work of David Hill, an English Methodist missionary, during the Northern China drought in 1879. After his conversion he actively engaged in evangelism and

in running opium rehabilitation centres. Four of the 'Cambridge Seven' joined Pastor Hsi in Pingyang in 1885 to support his work there.

'Mr Hsi was ordained pastor of no particular district,' recorded Stanley Smith. 'He has done such an extensive work, and been so owned of God, that it was thought best that he should be free to go anywhere for the work of God in these parts, knowing well how he would be welcomed by all the churches.'[22] In August 1886, Hudson Taylor travelled to Shanxi for the first time, where he ordained Pastor Hsi.

Pastor Hsi and Dixon Hoste worked closely together until Pastor Hsi's death in 1896. Dr Martyn Lloyd Jones, in the foreword to the biography of Pastor Hsi by Geraldine Taylor, wrote of the Chinese convert and evangelist: 'The outstanding characteristic was his spirituality. He was truly a man of God in the real sense of the word. His simple, childlike faith which yet was strong and unshakable was astonishing. He took the New Testament as it was and put it into practice without any hesitations or reservations.'[23]

Above:
The 'Cambridge Seven' and (top) in traditional Chinese dress

China Council

In order to help John Stevenson in his new capacity as deputy director, the China Council was established at the Anqing meeting in November 1886. It consisted of experienced workers including John Stevenson (deputy director), James Broumton (treasurer), James Meadows (superintendent of Zhejiang Province), James Williamson (deputy superintendent) and William Cooper (superintendent of Anhui Province).

Below:
The China Council

Two important decisions were made at the first meeting: to call for 100 new missionaries and to establish a language school and office at Anqing. The document *CIM Principles and Practices* was also published as a result of this first meeting.

Missionary women in China

Many women were involved in the mission; for example, Jennie Taylor (née Faulding) was an incredible support to Hudson Taylor and a committed and industrious missionary in her own right. Also Emily Blatchley, who acted as a guardian to Hudson Taylor's children in England, played a vital role in the running of the mission in London, including editing the *Occasional Paper*, until her early death in July 1874. Another woman, Elizabeth Wilson, who spent 12 years in China from the comparatively mature age of 50, enabled women to travel alone into the interior with her on account of the reverence and respect afforded her by her grey hair! It is interesting to note that of the 100 that joined the mission in 1887, 58 were women, the majority unmarried.

Right:
Elizabeth Wilson

Between 1886 and 1890 over 30 women missionaries were sent to the Guangxin River region, including Katie Mackintosh and Jeanie Gray, who pioneered work in Yushan.[24] The impact of this 'women's work' reached well beyond the mission fields of the Guangxin River.

> '*With its native pastor and evangelists, its churches, schools, teachers, and scores of unpaid workers, with more than three thousand, five hundred believers baptized from the commencement, and thirty foreign missionaries all of whom are women, that chain of stations is unique in China and perhaps in any mission field... by its confirmation of Mr Taylor's convictions and the lines on which he and his fellow workers were acting, it has inspired and strengthened similar efforts in many other places.*'[25]

Hudson Taylor was quite radical in his approach to women on the mission field. Appeals for missionaries were made through publications, speaking engagements and personal invitation, and all those who came forward were considered but not necessarily accepted. His policy was 'willing, skilful workers' and this meant men and women. The ministry offered by women was considered a vital one, and also a necessary one given the shortage of men. Some were from wealthy families but they would have gone out in the same way as the men – living and working by faith.

'Cast upon God'

'God's work was not meant to be stationary, but always advancing,' said Hudson Taylor. For the leader of the mission, it really was 'time versus eternity'. And when Hudson Taylor looked back, many years later, over all the ways in which God had led him, 'he was impressed with the fact that every important advance in the development of the Mission had sprung from, or been directly connected with, times of sickness or suffering which had cast him in a special way upon God'.[26] In the Bible, Paul had come to the same realisation: 'But He said to me, "My grace is sufficient for you, for my power is made perfect in weakness." Therefore I will boast all the more gladly about my weaknesses, so that Christ's power may rest on me' (2 Corinthians 12:9).

Reflection – The fruit of the Spirit

'But the fruit of the Spirit is love, joy, peace, forbearance, kindness, goodness, faithfulness, gentleness and self-control.' *(Galatians 5:22–3)*

In chapter 8, we read about Hudson Taylor's 'personal Pentecost', an experience that led him to enjoy a deeper realisation of Christ's love and power. This was possibly his most important spiritual experience after his conversion. He called this 'the exchanged life', a life that *rested* in Christ alone. Hudson Taylor was being led by God step by step, not just practically but spiritually. From his early years as a Christian he had learnt to *trust* God. The next step was *dependence*. Then it was *rest*.

God had an incredible task for Hudson Taylor. It required an incredible faith. The man God had called to this task could not do it in his own strength. The spiritual depths to which God was leading Hudson Taylor was vital preparation for the increasingly demanding work ahead of him. It was Christlike work, requiring Christ-like love, joy, peace, patience, kindness, goodness, faithfulness, gentleness and self-control – the fruit of the Spirit. This fruit was evident in the lives of all those who joined the CIM, but Hudson Taylor had the added responsibility of leadership.

Christ was Hudson Taylor's Saviour; He was also his example. In word and deed, Hudson Taylor sought to demonstrate that Christlike love and compassion that we read about in the Bible. Consider Christ's example on the road to Emmaus; the story of the prodigal son; the woman at the well; the woman caught in adultery; the thief on the cross. Christ showed His love through gentleness, compassion, and honesty. He held eternity in view. He wanted people to know that He was the Son of God so that they might see and believe. Through word and through deed,

Christ showed His love for the world.

Just as Christ was Hudson Taylor's example, Hudson had to be an example for all those who joined the CIM. This was an incredible responsibility, and Hudson Taylor felt it keenly. How did he manage such a task? By living close to God, by being open to *His* will and to *His* Spirit. Hudson Taylor did not do anything in his own strength. We are told that he was 'lame in gait and little in stature', that he 'compelled Christian people to revise their idea of greatness'. He was not the big, charismatic, powerful personality that we perhaps expect of a leader. Instead we read that it was his 'sympathy and naturalness' that attracted men to him; that 'Taylor was able to command loyalty through his warmth, sensitivity and servant spirit to others'; and of many examples of personal sacrifice in his care for others.

Hudson Taylor's personal Pentecost had led him deeper into fellowship with God. It had also gifted him on a deeper level with the fruit of the Spirit, qualities that made him more Christlike but at the same time more human. It is this Spirit that Christ left with us on earth, a source of power and a gift of Christlike humanity that is available to all those who take up their cross and truly follow Him.

認為 Think

'The power given is not a gift from the Holy Spirit. He himself is the power. Today He is as truly available and as mighty in power as He was on the day of Pentecost. But since the day of Pentecost, has the whole church ever put aside every other work and waited upon Him for ten days that the power might be manifested? We give too much attention to method, and to machinery, and to resources, and too little to the source of power.'

Hudson Taylor spoke these words at the Ecumenical Missionary Conference in New York, just five years before his death. He was speaking with nearly 50 years' experience of worldwide mission. His personal Pentecost had been a defining moment in his own life. The power of the Spirit had become a living and powerful reality for him from that moment on. Those words, spoken in 1900, convey one of the most important lessons Hudson Taylor had learnt in his lifetime of service, a message that he wanted to share with the Church and the world: 'Perhaps the greatest hindrance to our work is our own imagined strength.' Do you give space and time for the Spirit's work in your life, your church, your mission?

響應 Respond

'We are not immediately appealing for new workers', wrote Hudson Taylor to the leaders of the Keswick Convention in 1897 with regard to the CIM. 'Our first need being to prepare for them in China, and the most important preparation of all a spiritual one.'

Spiritual growth is far more important than any other growth. If we are not spiritually strong as individuals or as a church, we are not strong enough to grow in any other way: 'to evangelize successfully the church must become a spiritual church.'[27] The priority of church should be to grow in faith together, and our priority as individuals is to draw nearer to God. This is foundational to all other growth. How true is this for you and your church?

> 'It is a far greater triumph for Christ to put a man right than to get rid of him. Though we cannot scold them into right, we may often love them into right.'

Chapter 10

AN INTERNATIONAL MISSION

(1888–1899)

'On eagles' wings'

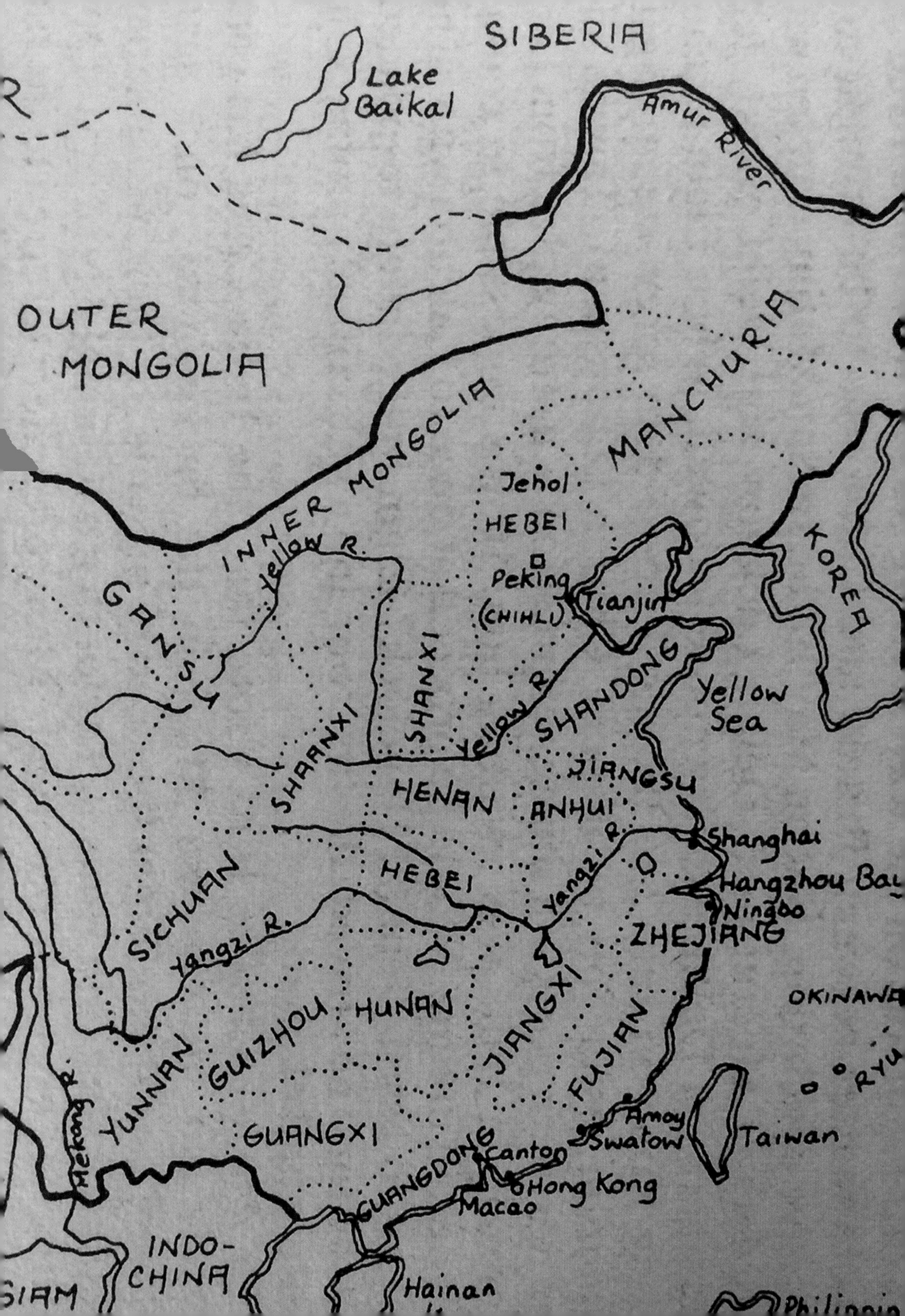

SIBERIA

Lake Baikal

Amur River

OUTER MONGOLIA

INNER MONGOLIA

MANCHURIA

KOREA

Jehol

HEBEI

Peking (CHIHLI)

Tianjin

Yellow R.

GANSU

Yellow R.

SHANXI

SHANXI

SHANDONG

Yellow Sea

SHAANXI

HENAN

JIANGSU

ANHUI

Yangzi R.

Shanghai

Hangzhou Bay

Ningbo

ZHEJIANG

SICHUAN

HEBEI

Yangzi R.

Yangzi R.

GUIZHOU

HUNAN

JIANGXI

FUJIAN

OKINAWA

YUNNAN

GUANGXI

GUANGDONG

Amoy

Swatow

Taiwan

RYU

Mekong R.

Canton

Hong Kong

Macao

INDO-CHINA

Hainan

Philippines

SIAM

The years 1888–1899 witnessed significant expansion of the China Inland Mission (CIM) and gospel work in China in a manner and means far beyond Hudson Taylor's dreams or expectations. It is worth remembering that when Hudson Taylor first set sail for China, he did not think he would even see his homeland again. However, he had put his faith and trust in the living God, and in his lifetime, Hudson not only sailed to China a total of 11 times, he also travelled extensively in the United Kingdom, the United States of America, Canada, India, Australia, New Zealand, Scandinavia, Germany, Switzerland and France. He was keen to work with other mission agencies at home and abroad to enable the gospel to be 'proclaimed to every creature under heaven' (Colossians 1:23). Though up to this point, Hudson did not envisage the expansion of the CIM to incorporate international branches – in fact, initially, he was very much against it.

'An ascending plane'[1]

The first suggestion of an international mission came at the close of 1887, with a visit to the CIM headquarters in Pyrland Road by an American, Henry Frost. Frost had been in correspondence for some time with Benjamin Broomhall and had come to London to talk with Hudson Taylor about the establishment of an American branch of the CIM. He, and others, had strongly felt God's guidance in this matter, so it came as quite a surprise to find Hudson Taylor very much against the idea. Hudson's feeling was that a transplanted mission, like a transplanted tree, would have difficulty taking root in the new soil – a fresh organisation would be better.

Despite the disappointment and confusion felt by Frost at Hudson's response, their meeting proved to be the start of an abiding friendship, stemming from a deeply spiritual connection and shared passion for mission. When Frost heard that Hudson Taylor was planning on returning to China and would be willing

Left:
Map showing
provinces
of China

to visit America en route, if invited, he wasted no time informing friends, including the evangelist, Dwight Moody. Invitations soon began to reach England, and at the end of June 1888, Hudson Taylor, with his son Howard, set sail on board the *S.S. Etruria* for what was to be the first of five visits to North America.

Right:
Howard and
Geraldine Taylor

Over the next three months, they travelled extensively throughout the United States and Canada.[2] A great deal of financial support was given in support of the mission, and a number of new candidates were interviewed and accepted. When Hudson Taylor set sail from Canada early in October 1888, he took with him the first party of American missionaries, and left behind a vast army of people generously supporting the mission in both prayer and provision. Though brief, Hudson was kept busy during this trip with many speaking engagements, providential connections and timely answers to prayer as these eye-witness accounts reveal:

'When he came to Northfield and appealed on behalf of China, the hearts of the delegates burned within them. And he not only made the needs of the mission-field very real; he showed us the possibilities of the Christian life... His addresses were so much appreciated that Mr Moody had to announce extra meetings... Eternity alone can reveal the results of that life, and the effect of his words upon our Student Movement.' (Robert Wilder)

'Hearts and lives were brought into an altogether new relationship to God and Christ, and not a few, in the joyfulness of full surrender, quietly but finally offered themselves to the Lord for His service anywhere and everywhere.' (Henry Frost)

*'It was a meeting never to be forgotten, and money for the
China Inland Mission came in without any advertisement
or urging on the part of any.' (Dr W.J. Erdman)*

*'Sunday night, 23 September 1888, saw the greatest and most
enthusiastic gathering ever held in Toronto up to that time.
The place was the YMCA, the hour 8.30pm... to hear the
Rev. J. Hudson Taylor and the men and women accepted by
him for work in China. The power of God was manifest in a
wonderful way, and as a result a great and abiding impetus
was given to foreign missions.'[3]*

A temporary council, based in Toronto, was formed just before
Hudson Taylor left for China, with honorary secretaries in
Canada (Alfred Sandham) and the United States (Henry Frost).
This was a hugely significant step, one which Hudson Taylor
'assuredly gathered' to be the will of God. But it was an 'advance'
not foreseen by him, and one which he confessed to finding
incredibly daunting: 'I never felt more timid about anything in
my life', he said of this development.[4]

'Experience', wrote Howard and Geraldine Taylor, 'had taught
him that for every time of prosperity and blessing one of a special
trial was in store.'[5] The following months were indeed filled with
'wave after wave of trial',[6] not unexpected given the blessings
in America, but still incredibly difficult. 'Satan is raging', wrote
Hudson to his wife in February 1889. 'He sees his kingdom
attacked all over the land, and the conflict is awful.' Four mission
workers died within a month of him arriving in China and more
were to follow, alongside prolonged sickness and trials of other
kinds. In London, members and friends of the London Council
were expressing concern at the developments in North America
and the authority placed in the hands of the China Council.
Some were even contemplating resigning. 'Everything seemed
crowded into those terrible months', wrote the deputy director,
John Stevenson. It was a critical time for the mission.

Hudson Taylor's first recourse was to God. 'This is the greatest trial we have yet had,' he wrote to his wife in March 1889, 'it will bring the greatest blessing. Now the Lord has taken the burden off my shoulders, and He is going to order the whole thing. It is His work, not mine.' Then he took action. A passage home was booked. But when Hudson Taylor arrived in England in May 1889, he found, to his great surprise and relief, issues resolved and 'the stone already rolled away'. In a letter to John Stevenson at the end of May he wrote, 'I think that all may now be put right and that great good will result from our great trial'; and in July, 'I do not think things have been so cordial for years'. Such a spirit paved the way for further important developments at home: a deed of incorporation for the safeguarding of mission property was drawn up, several new members joined the London council, an auxiliary council was formed in Glasgow and a ladies council was formed in London.

In July 1889, Hudson Taylor took a return trip to North America. He stayed five months and in that time addressed over 40 meetings in 18 different centres, including the Niagara Conference and Northfields. Such was the welcome that Hudson Taylor received that Dwight Moody offered his 'Northfield Hotel' as a training centre for mission candidates during the winter months. Moody was also a Bible tutor at the centre and Henry Frost became the new treasurer and secretary, giving up a very comfortable home in New York to live in complete dependence upon God in Toronto. It was a time of both consolidation and advance: financial gifts far exceeded those of the previous year, old friendships were deepened and many new ones were formed. All these things enabled Hudson Taylor to sail for England much cheered and strengthened.

Below:
Training centre in Toronto

The next 16 months saw many more advances. In November 1889, Hudson Taylor visited Sweden, Norway and Denmark. In February 1890, a new headquarters for the CIM was opened in Shanghai, and in April the first Australian worker arrived in China. June saw the formation of the German China Alliance. In August, Hudson Taylor, accompanied by Montagu Beauchamp (one of the 'Cambridge Seven'), visited Australia for the first time to meet the Australian Council (formed in May 1890), returning to China in December with more Australasian workers.

Above: New CIM headquarters in Shanghai

But perhaps the most significant development was a new depth of vision experienced by Hudson while visiting the home of Jennie's father in Hastings. 'I confess with shame', he wrote a few months later, 'that the question, what did our Lord *really mean* by His command to, 'preach the Gospel to every creature' had never been raised by me. I had laboured for many years to carry the Gospel further afield as have many others; had laid plans for reaching every unevangelised province and many smaller districts in China, without realising the plain meaning of our Saviour's words.'[7]

These words became, for Hudson Taylor, a divine command. 'It was a question of duty, and no time was to be lost.' In December 1889, *China's Millions*, the mission magazine, included 'an earnest, practical paper entitled *To Every Creature*... Its plea was for immediate action... the united simultaneous action of all the societies that alone could put one thousand evangelists in the field without delay.'[8]

It was not only China that was in his vision, but the whole world: 'Could China be blessed alone? Would not the whole world necessarily share in the blessing? For we could not be blessed on the field without our home churches being brought into it; and if they were filled with spiritual life, every land would be thought of and cared for. The Church is well able to evangelise the whole world and to do it with rapidity.'[9] *To Every Creature* was now a literal command. When Hudson Taylor preached the opening sermon at the second General Missionary Conference in Shanghai in May 1890, he issued a call for 1,000 new workers for China in the next five years.

'On eagles' wings'

From 1 January to 12 April 1891, seven missionary parties from Europe, North America and Australia arrived in China, making a total of 78 new workers – the first of the 1,000 prayed for. This number included two groups from the newly formed Scandinavian China Alliance who arrived, full of enthusiasm, within three weeks of each other.

Above:
Scandinavian missionaries

But while the new missionaries brought great encouragement, there were also significant challenges for the mission in China, which Hudson Taylor had sole responsibility for as John Stevenson was on a much-needed furlough. Serious and widespread danger in the form of anti-foreign riots meant many mission premises were threatened, and some destroyed. 'I look on the recent riots as Satan's reply for the Conference appeal for a thousand additional workers,' he wrote to Hobart some months later. 'God will have His response, however; and while the enemy is mighty, God alone is almighty.'

His chief concern at this time was that the mission should stand for real faith during such a conflict, setting an example of quietness and confidence in God, especially to the Chinese Christians. In a circular letter, dated 17 June 1891, Hudson Taylor wrote: 'Moreover their sympathy will be drawn out towards us when they see us willing to suffer for the Gospel, as they so often have to do. A time of danger is a grand opportunity for being an object-lesson to the native Christians.'

The anti-foreign feeling died down after five dangerous months, the rebels dispersed by the heavy rains which followed a long and intensely hot summer – another answer to specific prayer. However, the ending of the internal troubles did not alleviate the burden of the '*ordinary* responsibilities and the pecuniary claim of a mission now approaching five hundred in number'. Hudson Taylor was writing to the home director Theodore Howard in London but, as ever, his worries were immediately followed by reassurances of the faithfulness of God. 'There is just one way to avoid being overwhelmed,' he wrote, 'to bring everything as it arises to our Master; and He does help, and He does not misunderstand.'

Another matter that was still to be agreed by the whole mission was whether the China Council should hold supreme headship. This was not a traditional approach to mission and many were doubtful, though Hudson Taylor was not. 'Evils far more serious would result from abandoning what I am convinced are God-given lines for the CIM', he wrote in a letter to Theodore Howard. Agreement was not immediate, but once again Hudson was able to perceive the hand of God in the delay, trusting as ever that 'God's clock keeps good time'. 'The Lord doubtless has his purpose in permitting it,' he wrote to John Stevenson at the close of 1891, 'and to learn any lesson He may have to teach us is more important than getting rid of the trouble.'

The years 1892 to 1894 brought with them many great encouragements. Henry Frost visited China for the first time, accompanying previous visitors Archibald and Mrs Orr-Ewing

Below:
Theodore Howard, Home Director, CIM

Above:
Walter B. Sloan, Junior Secretary, CIM

and Walter B. Sloan (later to become junior secretary of the mission in London). Hudson Taylor travelled to Vancouver and then onto London, visiting Keswick in July 1892.

In 1893, the China Council was at last recognised as the supreme head of the CIM, and Hudson Taylor made two visits to Germany in April and August. The following year, Hudson, Jennie and Geraldine Guinness sailed for China, stopping briefly in the United States to speak at the Students' Conference in Detroit, before arriving in Shanghai in April. It was here, not long after, that his son, Howard, married Geraldine Guinness. Howard and Geraldine remained very close to Hudson and Jennie, a closeness which enabled them, in later years, to complete with real depth of knowledge and understanding, the extensive and deeply personal two-volume biography of Hudson Taylor's life and work: *Hudson Taylor and the China Inland Mission: Growth of a Soul* and *Growth of a Work of God*.

Above:
Picture of Hudson Taylor taken in Keswick

After a short honeymoon, the young couple found themselves accompanying Hudson and Jennie on a long and dangerous trip through the heart of China. Serious complications had arisen, which threatened the recall of all Scandinavian missionaries from the inland provinces. A small band of missionaries (not CIM) had unwittingly commenced evangelistic work in ways that were 'foreign to native ideas of propriety'. Hudson Taylor had no choice but to delay his return to England and use his authority to help resolve the matter. Summer 1894, therefore, witnessed this small group of missionaries travelling through the interior with J.J. Coulthard (husband of Hudson's daughter, Maria) as escort. Five provinces and all the mission stations along the route were visited, with warm welcomes at each, especially for the 'Venerable Chief Pastor'. The Scandinavian problems were not only resolved, but even closer ties forged between the

Scandinavian Alliance workers and the CIM. Then, in July, there was a wonderful opportunity of a few days rest with Pastor Hsi, his wife and their dear friend and co-worker, Dixon Hoste. The Taylors were given a special suite of apartments – actually a simple barn temporarily transformed for their visit – by Pastor Hsi. It was while here that the Taylors learnt of the outbreak of war between China and Japan, meaning another delay in their hoped-for return to the work in England.

A forward movement

The year 1895 brought with it the fulfilment of the appeal for the 1,000 workers. A total of 1,153 new workers had been added to the mission field in China, from 45 different mission societies. Of these, only 480 were men, and, as the majority of societies worked mainly in the coastal provinces, this meant the needs of the inland provinces went mainly unanswered. On his sixty-third birthday, the war now over, Hudson sent out a new call, this time for 'large and immediate reinforcements', and for 'united prayer'. 'Never before', he wrote, in a circular letter from Shanghai on 21 May 1895, 'were we so well prepared for definite advance, and our hope and prayer is that now the war is over we may have given to us many "willing, skilful" helpers, men and women, for every department of missionary service.'

Hudson Taylor was hopeful; the command to reach 'every creature' instilled in his heart as he planned 'A Forward Movement'. [10] But the political situation in China was in crisis. With the ending of the war in April, China had been forced into a period of transition from her 'exclusive policy of centuries' to the inevitable acceptance of her place in 'the family of nations'. [11] The change was not going to take place easily, and foreigners were an obvious target. The next few months brought new and terrible waves of trial: mission stations were destroyed, homes pillaged, families forced to flee, and 'work that had taken long years to build up threatened with complete devastation'. Secret societies rose up, and disbanded Chinese soldiers became a serious menace, leaving Hudson Taylor seriously concerned, particularly for the hundreds of fellow-workers in the inland mission stations.[12]

The workers of the CIM were spared, but others were not. When news broke, on 1 August, of the cold-blooded murders of 11 workers of the Church Missionary Society (CMS), including women and children, 'the realisation came home to many a heart that a new era had dawned that day, and that a great price might yet have to be paid for the triumph of the Gospel in China'. But this did not deter the mission societies, nor the workers. A meeting in Exeter Hall, London, was held to pray for China and seek God's guidance as to the future of missionary work in that land. The secretary of the CMS 'expressed the conviction of all present when he said that it simply demonstrated China's unutterable need of the gospel, and was thus a call and a challenge to *advance*'. And at the end of October, Hudson Taylor, in a letter to the superintendent of Kansu Province, wrote, 'I am almost hourly praying that God will give more souls this winter than have ever been given before in the north-west.' Hudson Taylor knew from experience, as did his fellow-workers, that a time of trial was also a time of blessing. He was not wrong.

'The encouragements of the year 1895 were also great and many', wrote Dr and Mrs Howard Taylor. After a visit to the training homes, Hudson Taylor was able to write 'never have parties of brighter, more capable, more consecrated workers gone out from these homes than this year.' The work at Chefoo had grown rapidly, with over 20,000 outpatients visiting the dispensary annually; and money had been given for the building of a much-needed senior boys' school. When the building was completed, the superintendent of the station was compelled to say: 'Truly, the history of this school proves that God answers prayers, and that miracles are not doubtful events of a by-gone age of superstition.'

Another encouragement occurred when Rev Cassels (one of

the 'Cambridge Seven' and consecrated bishop in Western China) and Pastor Wang, both still devoted to the cause of Christ in China, travelled to Shanghai earlier that year to deliver a sum of $1,000 for the mission. This money had been put aside by Pastor Wang and his wife for their daughter, but their daughter and son-in-law (Pastor Wang's co-pastor in Hangzhou) had refused to accept it, desiring, instead, that it be used to support missionaries. The visit and the gift were both deeply moving to all at mission headquarters in Shanghai.

As Hudson Taylor looked back over the events of that year, he wrote: 'In the midst of our sorrows God has been working and it is no small joy to record that, notwithstanding all hindrances, and in some cases through the very trials reported, many souls have been brought to Christ, so that a larger number of converts have been baptized in 1895 than in any previous year.'

Above:
Bishop Cassels

'All One in Christ'

By 1896, the CIM was a society of over 700 interdenominational workers. These 'willing, skilful' workers included doctors, nurses, teachers, financial experts, stenographers, architects, land surveyors and even a bishop. 'We are a very large family, and rather mixed,' wrote William Cooper, assistant deputy director in China, 'but all labouring in blessed harmony in this work of works. With a bond of union like this and a field like China, we can afford to sink our differences.'

But for some, the interdenominational nature of the CIM caused concern. Hudson Taylor, however, was clear on this point when questioned during a visit to Berlin in 1897: 'The great work of the mission field, which is a call to us all, overrides theological differences, and our motto remains "All One in Christ".' The

CIM's Statement of Faith ensured unity in the essentials, and it is a measure of the man, and the mission strategy, that the work was able to advance 'in blessed harmony', given there must have been diversity of theological beliefs outside of these essentials.

One of the most significant advances during this time was the opening of the new CIM headquarters in Newington Green, London, which Hudson and Jennie saw for the first time in May 1896. Though quite simple, the building was able to accommodate guests – one of Hudson Taylor's cherished

Above:
CIM headquarters in Newington Green, London

ambitions – and over the door to the meeting hall, carved in stone, were the meaningful words, 'Have Faith in God'. Benjamin Broomhall, still nearby in Pyrland Road, had retired after 20 years of devoted service and Walter Sloan was now in post. This was a new era for the mission in London.

Worldwide, the CIM was an ever-expanding international mission. From 1896 to 1897, Hudson Taylor visited India (to speak at the Christian Student Conference in Calcutta), Germany (three times), Sweden, Norway, France (to visit William Berger, for what was to be their last meeting on earth), Switzerland (for much-needed rest) Theodore Howard and America (en route to China). Not only was the mission expanding geographically and in number of workers, it was also receiving financial 'showers of blessing'. In the summer of 1897, while Hudson and Jennie were enjoying the fresh mountain air of Switzerland, two significant donations were given: one for £10,000 for the general fund, and a very generous legacy of £100,000 for evangelistic and education work. Such gifts, Hudson Taylor believed, were confirmation of the divine command to proclaim the gospel 'to every creature', and a reminder of the work still to do in the vast – but now not forgotten – land of China.

It was with mixed emotions, therefore, that Hudson Taylor and Jennie sailed for China, in November 1897. They were thankful for the financial blessings and shared a renewed passion for future advances, but there was also sadness. They had just learnt that Hudson's daughter, Maria, had died in in Hangzhou, Zhenjiang, China at just 30 years old. Maria had been married to John Coulthard, a CIM missionary, and they had three children. She died shortly after her youngest child succumbed to dysentery. Maria had been instrumental in leading many Chinese women to faith in Christ during her short life as a missionary.

Finishing touches

Hudson Taylor reached Shanghai in January 1898, full of fire for a 'forward movement', a movement in which Chinese Christians would be instrumental. Native Chinese missionaries, preferably unmarried and with strong faith and spirituality, would work as itinerant evangelists for five years. However, 'spirit-filled missionaries' of any nationality were still needed, and Hudson eagerly looked forward to the forthcoming Keswick deputation, due to arrive in China later that year.

Unknown to Hudson and Jennie, however, God was bringing their own work in the field to a close and putting His 'finishing touches' to their life-long labours in China. From 1898 to 1899, Hudson met with the mission leaders seven times and resolved long-term problems, witnessed many souls saved and baptised, and heard the news that four stations had been established in Hunan (the last inland province to be evangelised). Hudson Taylor was confined to bed for much of this time, but as ever he saw a higher purpose at work. 'Sometimes God can carry on His work better without us than with us,' he wrote in April 1898.

The political situation was reaching crisis point. Hostilities were directed particularly towards missionaries. In the November edition of *China's Millions*, Henry Frost encouraged the mission with the following words: 'Leave God out of count, and fear might well possess and overwhelm us. Bring God into account and there is perfect peace for us at home and for our beloved missionaries in China. Satan is mighty, but God is almighty.'

Above:
Map showing Chongqing (also known as Chungking) in Sichuan Province

For 32 years God had protected His workers in the field, and not one life had been lost through violence or accident. But in November 1898, as Hudson and Jennie travelled across China to the West China Missionary Conference in Chongqing, Sichuan, they were told of the first CIM martyr, an Australian, named William Fleming. These were sad tidings, but were met with the same unswerving response. 'It seems that God is about to test us with a new *kind* of trial,' wrote Hudson to John Stevenson on 22 November, 'surely we need to gird on afresh "the whole armour of God". Doubtless it means fuller blessing, but through deeper suffering.' This was, indeed, a small foretaste of much deeper suffering to come for the mission.

The West China Missionary Conference proved a time of great blessing, but planned visits to many of the western stations had to be abandoned due to political unrest and Hudson's ill health. However, they were able to visit Hangzhou, Yantai (Chefoo) in late spring, where they watched the games and celebrations of the Chefoo School Foundation Day, and Mokanshan in the summer; these brief visits blessed them both with warm fellowship and happy memories. The trip culminated with some time spent back in Shanghai. When Hudson and Jennie boarded the boat bound for Australia and New Zealand on 26 September, they had no idea that their own work in China was over, or of the supreme difficulties ahead.

Reflection – Unity

'Therefore if you have any encouragement from being united with Christ, if any comfort from his love, if any common sharing with the Spirit, if any tenderness and compassion, then make my joy complete by being like-minded, having the same love, being one in spirit and of one mind.'
(Philippians 2:1–2)

Hudson Taylor led an interdenominational, international mission. It crossed theological as well as cultural divides. Yet for the most part it was a united and harmonious organisation. How did he achieve this? When challenged with the exact same question on a visit to Berlin in 1897, Hudson's reply was that they were 'All One in Christ'. His one driving passion, as it was for all the workers of the CIM, was the saving of souls, particularly Chinese souls. Hudson knew the powerful reality of a relationship with a living God. He believed, without a shadow of a doubt, that Christ was the Son of God, sent by God to earth, to become human and die on the cross that we might live. Christ was Hudson Taylor's Saviour and he wanted to share this vital gospel news with the Chinese.

Hudson Taylor was called by God to evangelise the whole of China. This was an enormous task and it required a harvest of 'willing, skilful workers'. They did not need degrees or qualifications in theology but a passion for souls, a personal relationship with the living God, knowledge of the Bible and a shared belief in the essentials of the Christian faith; this is what enabled the CIM to work together in unity. When missionaries were appointed to the CIM they all signed a Statement of Faith, so when disagreements or disputes arose, as they inevitably did, Hudson Taylor would remind the group of this Statement of Faith, the purpose of the mission and the motto, 'All One in Christ'.

Missionaries also undertook a rigorous training programme, set out in a short document explaining the principles and practices of the CIM. This included an intensive study of the Scriptures in both English and Chinese (and where necessary other languages and dialects), and a working knowledge of John Bunyan's *The Pilgrim's Progress* in Mandarin. The Statement of Faith and the training programme were both forthrightly evangelical. The missionaries' task was to evangelise the Chinese; theological differences outside the essentials were largely irrelevant to their mission. Discipleship in the main was to be left to the local Chinese churches set up by the missionaries. This was how and why it was possible to recruit missionaries from all denominations and still be a highly successful organisation. They were all united in the task of evangelisation and 'all one in Christ'.

Hudson Taylor believed that it was 'the right of all Christians to preach, baptise, and minister the Lord's supper.'[13] He believed in equality in evangelisation. This extended beyond denomination and education to gender, age and culture. Women and children needed the gospel too, so women (single and married) were necessary to mission work. Much of the fruit of the CIM came as a result of the tireless and sacrificial work of the women of the mission, both at home and in China.

It is, perhaps, Hudson Taylor's attitude to cross-cultural mission that he is most remembered for. Hudson Taylor did his best to become one of the Chinese. He was not the first missionary to adopt Chinese dress, but he was the first to lead a mission where this became a principle and practice for *all* workers on the field – men, women and children alike. Why was this important to Hudson Taylor? The reasons are best summed up in his own powerful, inspirational and heartfelt words:

'Why should such a foreign aspect be given to Christianity? The Word of God does not require it; nor, I conceive, could sound reason justify it. It is not their denationalization but their Christianization that we seek. We wish to see Christian Chinese men and women, true Christians, but withal true Chinese in every sense of the word. We wish to see churches of Christian Chinese presided over by Christian pastors and officers, worshipping in edifices of a thoroughly Chinese style of architecture... If we really desire to see the Chinese such as we have described, let us, as far as possible, set before them a correct example. Let us in everything not sinful become Chinese, that by all means we may win some. Let us adopt their costume, acquire their language, study to imitate their habits, and approximate to their diet as far as health and constitution will allow. Let us live in their houses, making no unnecessary alterations in external appearance. Knives and forks, plates and dishes, cups and saucers must give place to chopsticks, native spoons and basins.'[14]

Christianity is not a Western construct: neither is it an Eastern one. Its single identity is Christ. If we believe in the essentials of the Christian faith, then we are 'all one in Christ'. This is what enabled Hudson Taylor and the CIM to work in unity and in harmony, and to fulfil Christ's command to 'go and bear fruit – fruit that will last' (John 15:16).

認為Think

'The great work of the mission field, which is a call to us all, overrides theological differences, and our motto remains, "All One in Christ"' said Hudson Taylor speaking in Berlin in 1897. The CIM clearly set out the essentials of faith so that all members could work together, united in these essentials. Anything else was peripheral. This was how the mission was able to be interdenominational and united, with one overriding, God-given aim: to take the gospel 'to every creature' (Colossians 1:23).

The agreed essentials underpinning the Statement of Faith were: truth of Scripture, Trinity, sin and regeneration, atonement, justification by faith, the resurrection of the body and eternal life (heaven and hell). These shared fundamental principles enabled the CIM to work in harmony and become 'one of the great miracles of action in history'.

In our interdenominational, culturally diverse worldwide Church, is your passion for souls such that you can say, with Christlike love, as Hudson Taylor did, that we are 'all one in Christ'?

響應 Respond

'If the members are godly and wise, walking in the spirit of unity and love, they will not lack guidance in important matters and at critical times, but should another spirit prevail no rules could save the Mission nor would it be worth saving. The China Inland Mission must be a living body in fellowship with God or it will be of no further use and cannot continue.' (Taken from CIM's Statement of Faith.)

The CIM was God's work – the people simply channels – done in God's way, biblically, spiritually and prayerfully. It never lacked God's supplies because the work was in harmony with God's will. It was a *divinely* led, *divinely* driven and *divinely* resourced mission. Anything else, in Hudson Taylor's words, could not, and should not, continue.

This is quite a strong line to take but one worth considering. Do we sometimes continue with a church group or project even when it becomes clear that God is no longer at the centre of it? Is there a challenge here for your own church, fellowship or mission?

'All One in Christ.'

Chapter 11

'IT IS MINE'

(1900–1905)

'Life immortal'

Hudson and Jennie Taylor left Australia and New Zealand early in 1900, bound for the United States of America and the New York Ecumenical Conference, which promised to be 'the greatest of all missionary gatherings'. At the opening meeting on 21 April, 2,500 people were packed into Carnegie Hall. Seated on the front row of the platform was: the future President, Theodore Roosevelt; the former President, Benjamin Harrison; and Hudson Taylor. In his opening address, the then current President, William McKinley, spoke these words:

> 'I am glad of the opportunity to offer without stint a tribute of praise and respect to the mission effort which has wrought such wonderful triumphs for civilization. The story of the Christian missions is one of thrilling interest and marvellous results... Wielding the sword of the Spirit, they have conquered ignorance and prejudice... They have been among the pioneers of civilization. Who can estimate their value to the progress of nations? Their contribution to the onward and upward march of humanity is beyond all calculation.'[1]

During the conference, many prayers were focused on China, where the situation was becoming desperate. Hudson and Jennie remained in North America after the conference but a heavy work schedule there and worry about events in China were too much for the already weary Hudson and he suffered a serious breakdown. He was, quite simply, 'worn out with loving'.[2] He loved China and the Chinese with a spiritual passion, and the hundreds of missionaries working with him on the field and at home were counted as family. Many stories are told of his faithfulness to this extended family including crossing mountains to care for a sick child, the adoption of a child whose missionary parents had died, checking on sick patients throughout the night, daily praying for each missionary by name, and waking before sunrise to present the needs of China and the mission before his heavenly Father. Jesus Christ was Hudson Taylor's Saviour *and* his example. The words of John Stevenson, writing in 1889, sum up the 'great-heart' of the man who had been called by God into the heart of the dragon:

'Oh, his was a life worth looking into – searching through and through! Get a man like Mr Taylor, and you could start any mission tomorrow. It was most wonderful – his life. I never knew any other so consistent; and I watched him year in and year out, and had exceptional opportunities for doing so. He walked with God; his life bore the light all through. And he was so gracious and accessible! Day or night, literally at all hours, he was ready to help in sickness or any trouble. For self-denial and practical consecration, one could not but feel, he stood alone.'

Right:
James Hudson Taylor with John Stevenson and James Meadows

It was this vast capacity for love and service which were to make the events of the next few months the supreme trial, not only for the CIM, but for Hudson Taylor himself.

The supreme trial

Hudson and Jennie reached England in June 1900, but almost immediately travelled on to Switzerland for a period of rest and recuperation, staying in a small pension in the alpine resort of Davos. It proved a fortuitous decision. Hudson was already very weak and would not have coped – either physically or emotionally – with the influx of telegrams to the headquarters in London, telling of the Boxer Uprising and the riots and massacres in station after station of the CIM. Anti-foreign feeling was at its height, with missionaries a particular target. Orthodox, Protestant and Catholic Christians were all subject to the same cruelty, hatred and violence. The 'deeper suffering' that Hudson had spoken of not two years earlier was now upon them. Some news from China did reach Davos, but Hudson, already 'worn out with loving', was almost unable to bear it. 'I cannot read,' he said, 'I cannot think; I cannot even pray; but I can trust.'

As the depth of the suffering became clear, Hudson's grief and agony was exacerbated by his own helplessness. His greatest desire at this time was to be in China, supporting the missionaries and suffering with them in their time of acute need. To be absent from the battle ground, forced to stand by and do nothing, this was Hudson's personal and supreme trial. 'If they could come to me in their sorrows and I could only weep with them, it might be a comfort to some,' he said, his thoughts with the refugees taking shelter in Shanghai. And later, to a family member, 'Yes, but it's hardest of all to do *nothing* for His sake.' For Hudson Taylor, the toughest sacrifice, the hardest labours, were as nothing compared to a position of helplessness.

More missionaries from the CIM were murdered during the Boxer Uprising than from any other mission agency; in total, the lives of 58 adults and 21 children were brutally brought to an end in the 'over-sweeping horror of that summer'. 'But in all the correspondence of the period,' wrote Howard and Geraldine Taylor, 'not one bitter feeling can be traced against their persecutors, not one desire for vengeance or even for indemnification. The spirit of that tender mother who – dying after weeks of brave endurance on the journey to Hankow, having lost one little boy by the way and witnessed the prolonged suffering of others – whispered to her husband, "How I wish I could have lived, I wish I could have gone back there, to tell the dear people more about Jesus", seemed rather to animate all hearts.'

Hudson's health deteriorated rapidly as news of the tragic events in China continued to flood in. 'Anguish of heart was killing him', wrote his daughter-in-law, 'it was only by keeping the tidings back in measure that the slender thread of life held on.' But as the 'Boxer madness' began to pass away, Hudson regained enough strength to cope with more detailed knowledge of what had taken place and take some charge of the situation. Upholding CIM principles, he directed that no offer of indemnity for losses sustained should be accepted, an action 'warmly approved' at the British Foreign Office. Neither had the tragic events dulled his, or others', fervour for mission. Letters and gifts flooded in, and in December that year Hudson Taylor received 'a letter of loving sympathy' from Shanghai, signed by 300 members of the mission. His loving response to the mission's most supreme of trials was:

'We thank God for the grace given to those who have suffered. It is a wonderful honour He has put upon us as a mission to be trusted with so great a trial, and to have among us so many counted as worthy of a martyr's crown... How much it has meant to us to be so far from you in the hour of trial we cannot express, but the throne of grace has been as near to us here as it would have been in China... May we all individually learn the lessons God would teach, and be prepared by His Spirit for any further service to which He may call us.'[3]

Once again, Hudson Taylor's answer to adversity was to 'advance'.

Life immortal

In the summer of 1901, Hudson Taylor suffered a fall while visiting Chamonix and a re-occurrence of his old spinal problems, putting to an end any thought of an imminent return to China. A few months later he and Jennie visited England, returning to Switzerland in the spring of 1902. This time, they rented a small apartment in a pension in the hamlet of Les Chevalleyres by Lake Geneva and near to the home of their beloved friend, Mary Berger. It had a little sitting room, a bedroom, a front balcony and a closed-in verandah, which faced the rising sun and nearby meadows. This was the closest they had ever had to a settled home, and precious time together brought much joy and 'quiet happiness'. The pension soon became 'a resort for English guests' and the little corner sitting room 'a CIM centre up among the mountains'.

Below: Hudson and Jennie Taylor in their apartment in Switzerland

'It was not so much what your father *said* but what he *was* that proved a blessing to me,' wrote one such visitor, who spent six

Above:
The pension in
Les Chevalleyres

months with the Taylors in Les Chevalleyres. 'You may remember the words of Emerson, "Common souls pay with what they do, nobler souls with what they are." Your father bore about with him the fragrance of Jesus Christ. His strong faith, quietness, and constant industry, even in his weakness, touched me deeply... To see a man who had been so active compelled to live a retired life, unable to pray more than minutes at a time, and yet remaining bright and even joyous, greatly impressed me. I remember his saying, "If God can afford to lay me aside from active service, surely I should not object." Not a single complaint or murmur did we ever hear from his lips. He was always cheerful – rejoicing in the flowers by day and studying the stars at night.'[4]

Three leaders of the mission were among the visitors to Les Chevalleyres in the autumn and winter of 1902 – Henry Frost, Walter Sloan and Dixon Hoste.[5] Hudson Taylor realised now that the time had come for him to step down as General Director of the mission and had for a while been prayerfully considering a suitable successor. Dixon Hoste's visit to Switzerland confirmed Hudson's leading, and, in January the following year (1903), Hoste formally took over the role. It was an appointment fully endorsed by all the directors and mission councils. 'I am thankful that you have been led to select, perhaps, the most prayerful man among us', wrote Mr Orr-Ewing. A new era in the history of the CIM had begun.

For the Taylors, this was also the beginning of a new, even quieter life. Though Hudson often felt the trial of standing aside and doing '*nothing* for His sake', he accepted it as all part of God's plan. Both Hudson and Jennie were approaching their final years on this earth, and time just to be still and quiet together in a beautiful setting, without the heavy responsibilities of the mission, can be viewed – with hindsight – as a precious gift from God to two devoted and faithful servants.

In July 1903, they learnt that Jennie was seriously ill with cancer, the same disease that had claimed her mother. The disease was too advanced for treatment so Hudson and Jennie spent the winter in Lausanne to be near the doctor, returning to their home in Les Chevalleyres in the spring. Jennie died peacefully in July 1904, her husband by her side.

Hudson Taylor stayed on at the pension, joined by his niece, Mary Broomhall, for company. A delegation of old friends from Toronto spent the winter with him, and with a significant improvement in his health, a trip to China, via the United States, was planned. This was Hudson's seventh visit to North America. His great interest was in the new centre of the mission in Philadelphia, where he spent almost a fortnight, accompanied by Howard and Geraldine Taylor. Then it was on to his beloved China.

In Loving Memory

OF

JANE ELIZABETH TAYLOR,

THE BELOVED WIFE OF THE

REV. J. HUDSON TAYLOR,

Who fell asleep on Saturday, July 30th 1904,

Aged 61 Years;

AT CHEVALLEYRES, VEVEY, SWITZERLAND.

Above: Memorium card for Jennie (Jane) Taylor

Hudson landed in Shanghai on 17 April 1905, where he was received with much love and thoughtfulness. Flowers filled his rooms, and many letters of love and sympathy flowed in. Old friends travelled to see him, and many hours were spent sharing memories of times past. Easter was spent at Yangzhou and then it was on to the new mission house at Zhenjiang. From here he was able to walk to the cemetery overlooking the river to visit the graves of his first wife, Maria, and four of his children (Gracie, Samuel, Noel and daughter Maria who died in 1897). Next stop was Hankow, where he was reunited with more old friends, before taking advantage of the new railway running north to Peking (Beijing) to visit five mission centres in the Hunan province.

After a quiet Sunday back in Hankow, Hudson decided to go by steamer to Changsa, the capital of Hunan, a province he had never visited.

Hunan was the first of all the inland provinces the mission had attempted to enter but the last in which it had been possible to settle:

Above:
Railroad in
Hunan province

'As they crossed the far-reaching lake and steamed up the river, passing well-built cities, beautiful pagodas and temples, rich plains covered with ripening crops, and noble mountain ranges near and distant, they could not but think of all the toil and prayer of years gone by, of buried lives and dauntless faith, richly rewarded at last in the change that was coming over the attitude of the people. Until eight or nine years previously there had not been one Protestant missionary settled in the province. None had been able to gain a footing. No fewer than a hundred and eleven missionaries were to be found there now, connected with thirteen societies, working in seventeen central stations and aided by a strong band of Chinese helpers.'[6]

Hudson, with Howard and Geraldine, reached Changsa on Thursday 1 June 1905. Friday was spent visiting the city, including the site for a planned new hospital. A reception for 'Inland China's Grace-man', as some affectionately called him, was held on the Saturday afternoon. Tea was served on the lawn and Hudson, seasonably dressed in a suit of Shantung silk, sat in the midst of the guests, enjoying the 'quiet, happy time'.

It was later that same evening, after he had retired to his room to rest, that Hudson Taylor quietly and peacefully passed away. He was in bed, a lamp burning on the chair beside him. Geraldine was sitting by his bedside, talking about the pictures in the copy of the *Missionary Review*, which was lying open on his bed. Hudson turned his head and gave a little gasp. Geraldine had barely time to call Howard to the bedside before his dear father drew his last breath. 'It was not death – but the glad, swift entry upon life immortal,' they wrote of that moment, 'And, oh, the look of rest and calm that came over the dear face was wonderful! The weight of years seemed to pass away in a few moments. The weary lines vanished. He looked like a child quietly sleeping, and the very room seemed full of unutterable peace.'[7]

Above: James Hudson Taylor having tea shortly before he passed away

Hudson Taylor's coffin was lovingly prepared by local people in Hunan, but the cemetery at Zhenjiang was where he was buried, next to the graves of his beloved wife and children. Just a little more than 73 years before, his parents, James and Amelia Taylor, had consecrated the life of their firstborn child to God. How precious now, the fulfilment of that divine assurance: '"*It is mine*", not for time only but for eternity.'[8] James Hudson Taylor had obeyed God's call on his life. It was now time for him to receive his crown and to rest, for all eternity, safe in the arms of Jesus.

Above:
James Hudson
Taylor's coffin
and funeral

Fruit that will last

*'You did not choose me, but I chose you and appointed you so
that you might go and bear fruit – fruit that will last – and so
that whatever you ask in my name the Father will give you.'
(John 15:16)*

James Hudson Taylor had been appointed by God to 'go and bear
fruit – fruit that will last'. In faith he had obeyed, and the legacy
he has left behind – in China and beyond – is an incredible one.
But Hudson Taylor was, to use his own words, simply 'the little
servant of an Illustrious Master'. It was God's work, done in
God's way, with God-given supplies. To God be the glory.

*'I will make them and the places surrounding my hill a blessing.
I will send down showers in season; there will be showers
of blessing.' (Ezekiel 34:26)*

'The vestibule of heaven'

'If God has called you to be really like Jesus in your spirit, He will draw you into a life of crucifixion and humility, and put on you such demands of obedience that He will not allow you to follow other Christians; and in many ways He will seem to let other good people do things that He will not let you do. Other Christians and ministers who seem very religious and useful may push themselves, pull wires and work schemes to carry out their plans, but you cannot do it; and if you attempt it, you will meet with such failure and rebuke from the Lord as to make you sorely penitent. Others may boast of themselves, of their work, of their success, of their writings, but the Holy Spirit will not allow you to do any such thing; and if you begin it, He will lead you into some deep mortification that will make you despise yourself and all your good works.

'Others may be allowed to succeed in making money, but it is likely that God will keep you poor, because He wants you to have something far better than gold, and that is helpless dependence upon Him, that He may have the privilege (the right) of supplying your needs day by day out of an unseen treasury. The Lord will let others be honoured and put forward, and keep you hidden away in obscurity, because He wants some choice fragrant fruit for His coming glory which can only be produced in the shade. He will let others do a work for Him and get the credit for it, but He will let you work and toil on without knowing how much you are doing; and then to make your work still more precious, He will let others get the credit for the work you have done, and this will make your reward ten times greater when Jesus comes.

'The Holy Spirit will put a watch over you, with a jealous love, and will rebuke you for little words and feelings or for wasting your time, over which other Christians never seem distressed. So make up your mind that God is an infinite Sovereign, and has the right to do as He pleases with His own, and He may not explain to you a thousand things which may puzzle your reason in His dealings with you. He

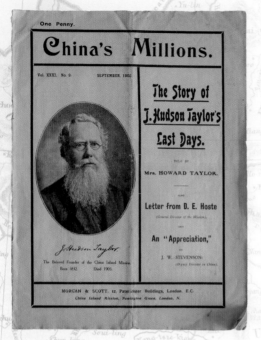

will take you at your word and if you absolutely sell yourself to be His slave, He will wrap you, but let other people say and do many things which He will not let you say or do.

'Settle it forever that you are to deal directly with the Holy Spirit, and that He is to have the privilege of tying your tongue, or chaining your hand, or closing your eyes, in ways He does not deal with others. Now when you are so possessed with the Living God, that you are in your secret heart pleased and delighted over the peculiar, personal, private, jealous guardianship of the Holy Spirit over your life, you will have found the vestibule of heaven.'[9]

Reflection – Heaven

'For to me, to live is Christ and to die is gain.'
(Philippians 1:21)

'If I had a thousand pounds China should have it – if I had a thousand lives China should have them. No! Not China, but Christ. Can we do too much for Him? Can we do enough for such a precious Saviour?'[10]

After his own conversion, Hudson Taylor was driven by a passion to share the gospel with everyone he came into contact with. But God had a special commission for him – to take the good news of Christ to the whole of China. Hudson realised this quite soon after becoming a Christian and from that moment on his whole life, as we have read, was focused on fulfilling this God-given task. In preparation he trained as doctor and midwife and along the way became a self-taught linguist, sailor, architect and builder. He was a radical disciple: a daring, courageous, pioneering, sacrificial follower of Christ. But in his own eyes, he was none of these. It was God who was the 'great designer' of both man and mission; God who was the power and the brains behind this incredible task. Hudson Taylor was simply 'the little servant of an illustrious Master'. So what was the secret of this small, insignificant Barnsley-born man? The weak child who even in adulthood was 'lame in gait; and little in stature'? Simply put, he held eternity in view.

'We dwell too much on the things that are seen and temporal and far too little on those that are unseen and eternal', wrote Hudson Taylor to his sister in March 1852. 'Only let us keep these things in view, and the cares and the pleasures of this world will not affect us much... Oh my dear Sister, let us live for eternity!' This was Hudson Taylor's secret, the key that enabled him to venture all for God and to lead such an abundant, fruitful life here on earth. He had laid down all claims on life here. His sight was set on an eternity with Christ his Saviour: 'a new heaven and a new earth' (Revelation 21:1), which the Bible promises to all those who take up their cross and follow Christ.

Hudson Taylor believed absolutely in the Word of God. For him the Bible was 'a book of certainties'. He had put it to the test and it had proved trustworthy and true. He believed that the words of Christ, 'I am going there to prepare a place for you' (John 14:2), were literally true. Heaven was a promise and a reality: a free gift from God through Christ to all those who believe. Eternity became his view, his focus. Here on earth he was simply a 'stranger in a strange land'. This is what freed him to live for Christ: to submit *everything* to His service and to the command, 'go and make disciples of all nations' (Matthew 28:19).

Left:
Cover of *China's Millions* in September 1905 following Hudson Taylor's death

Hudson Taylor was a man who lived for eternity – his own and others' – surrounded by an organisation made up of missionaries who also lived for eternity. This was the secret of the man and the mission – they lived for eternity.

認為 Think

In a letter to his sister Amelia written in March 1852, Hudson Taylor wrote: 'The value of a soul – how immense, incalculable! The precious blood of Christ was the only price at which it could be purchased, and that was not withheld. If we really believe these things and have received the blessings that flow from His sacrifice, shall we withhold ourselves, our loved ones from Him? Shall we fear to enter on His service because it will lessen our comforts?... Shall we count even our lives dear, if we may perchance win souls for Jesus? No, a thousand times, no!'[11]

Hudson Taylor lived for eternity. Knowing he had a personal assurance of salvation through a confession of faith in Christ as his Lord and Saviour meant Hudson was released to live a life resting in the love, the wisdom and the will of God. He could risk all, dare all, venture all, knowing that 'to live is Christ and to die is gain'. But to live for eternity was also to live with the eternity of others in view. Every man, woman and child was a soul needing to be saved: a soul that would pass into one of two eternities – a perfect eternity with God, or a terrible eternity without. It was this great heart for souls that informed every aspect of Hudson Taylor's life and mission. Do you live for eternity – your own *and* that of others?

響應 Respond

'For God so loved the world that he gave his one and only Son, that whoever believes in Him shall not perish but have eternal life.' *(John 3:16)*

This life is only temporary. We will all die. But the Bible teaches that there is a reward for all those who truly believe in Christ as the Son of God – heaven! This is the promise of a restored creation; 'a new heaven and a new earth' (Revelation 21:1) where God and man will live in perfect harmony forever. A place where there will be no more tears, suffering, evil, pain or fear. What an amazing reward and promise! It is a promise that Christ commands us to share with our family, our friends, our neighbours. It was what motivated Hudson Taylor – let it motivate us too.

'Love gave the blow that for a little while makes the desert more dreary, but heaven more home-like. "I go to prepare a place for you": and is not our part of the preparation peopling it with those we love?'[12]

How much do you value the souls of people you love? Read the words of Hudson Taylor above once more. What more can you do to 'people' heaven with those you love?

'Let us live for eternity!'

The Conversion of a Confucian Scholar

A leading Confucian scholar called Mr Nying, proud of his learning and position, would have nothing to do with foreign missionaries who from time to time came to preach strange doctrines in his city. But he was interested in Western science and so, taking advantage of one of John Stevenson's visits, he strolled along to the mission house and entered into conversation with the evangelist. After some discussion on the topics of Mr Nying's choice, Stevenson turned to the New Testament lying on the table, and quite naturally asked his visitor: 'Have you in your library the books of the Christian religion?'

'I have,' replied Mr Nying, 'but to be quite candid, I do not find them very interesting.'

There followed a conversation in which it appeared that Mr Nying was sceptical as to the existence of God or the soul, and thought prayer manifestly absurd.

'If there *were* a Supreme Being, he would be far too great and distant to take any notice of our little affairs,' he said.

Patiently Stevenson sought to bring him to a better point of view, but without success. So this is what he suggested: 'You say there is no God, and that even if there were He would never condescend to listen to our prayers: but believe me, if you go home tonight and take up that New Testament, and before opening it humbly and earnestly ask the God of Heaven to give you His Holy Spirit that you may understand it aright, that book will be a new book to you and will soon mean more than any other book in the world. Put it to the proof; and whether you pray for yourself or not, I will pray for you.'

More impressed than he cared to show, the scholar went home and did as he was told. 'O God, if there be a God, save my soul, if I have a soul. Give me Thy Holy Spirit, and help me to understand this book,' he prayed.

Hour after hour as he turned the pages, a new spirit was taking possession of him. His heart burned within him. The wonderful Saviour of whom he read was becoming real to him as he could never have believed possible. The words He had spoken long ago were living and powerful still. They searched him through and through, and brought not only a new awareness of sin, but peace and healing too. And, oh, the joy that began to well up within him!

For many days Mr Nying dared not confess his newfound faith to his wife, worried as to her response. But one evening, in desperation, he told her he had something to tell her. They sat in silence for a while. He had no idea what to say or where to begin, he just knew he must tell her. Then it all came out. To Mr Nying's surprise, his wife listened with growing wonder.

'Have you really found Him?' she broke in. 'Oh, I have so wanted to know! For there *must* be a living God! Who else could have heard my cry for help long, long ago?'

It was when the Taiping rebels had come to the city in which her parents lived, burning and pillaging everything. Their home had been ravaged like the rest. Many people were killed, many committed suicide, and she, helpless, had crept inside a wardrobe to hide. She heard the soldiers coming nearer and nearer. 'Oh Heavenly Grandfather, *save me!*' she had cried.

None but the true and living God could have answered that prayer. The rebels entered the room she was in but passed by the hiding place where she was crouching, scarcely daring to breathe. Ever since then she had so longed to know about *Him* – the wonderful God who had saved her.

With what joy and thankfulness her husband assured her not only that there was such a being – supremely great and good – but that He had spoken, had made Himself known to men! Did ever the story of redeeming love seem more precious, or heart rejoice to tell it forth more than that of the once-proud Confucian scholar as he began to preach Christ in his home and city? So fervent was his spirit that it disconcerted those who thought to laugh him out of his new-fangled notions.

Loving his Bible, and helped by visits to the local missionary station, Mr Nying soon became a preacher of much power. Among his first converts was a man who had been the terror of the neighbourhood. What power had turned the lion into a lamb the villagers could not tell, but the old father the man had formerly treated with cruelty and neglect could testify to the reality of the change, and, like his son, was soon a believer in Jesus.

In ever-widening circles the blessing spread, until it reached the keeper of a gambling-den and house of bad repute in a neighbouring town. His conversion was even more notable than the others, for it banished the gaming-tables, emptied the house of bad characters and turned his best and largest room into a chapel. It was his own idea to have it cleaned and whitewashed before offering it, free of cost, as a place of worship.

Ten altogether had followed Mr Nying in confessing Christ, and there were not a few interested enquirers. Upon Hudson Taylor's arrival in the city they began to drop in, until he found himself surrounded by this bright, earnest company of believers. And, oh, the rejoicing, the greetings and conversations, the singing and prayers! It was a little bit of heaven below – a precious foretaste of the hundredfold reward.

'I could have wept for joy,' Hudson Taylor wrote, 'to hear what grace had done for one and another of those present; and most of them could tell of some relative or friend of whose conversion they had good hope... I have never seen anything like it in China.'[13]

> 'There is a living God, He has spoken in the Bible. He means what He says, and will do all He has promised.'

Acknowledgements

Firstly, I must thank Peter Morden and Lynette Brooks for being instrumental in enabling me to write this book – Peter for the suggestion that I might be a suitable author, and Lynette for the invitation. The timing was perfect! Thank you.

I also wish to thank my mother, Audrey Broomhall, for reading the chapters through as I completed them and for her advice and encouragement based on years of reading and a wealth of knowledge on the subject. It is a real sadness to us as a family that Dad is not alive to share the journey. He would have been quietly proud of this opportunity to share the story of Hudson Taylor and our incredible spiritual heritage. And thanks to my niece, Laura Boland, who has not only been great company in the last couple of months as I have been engrossed in the research and writing, but who has also proofread the entire book and offered her objective, youthful and very constructive comment.

I am indebted to Marion Osgood, Tony Waghorn and the staff at OMF headquarters, Borough Green, for their contribution to the research and support for the project. Marion and Tony have both been brilliant in organising access to the archives and to the wonderful array of artefacts, photographs and publications available, and for just generally pointing me in the right direction – thank you! Also, a big thanks to OMF for permission to use these, as needed, in this book; they really help bring the story to life.

To everyone at CWR, especially Andrea Bodle (editor), Joanna Duke (designer) and Rebecca Berry. Thank you for your encouragement, enthusiasm and expertise, and for involving me in more than just the writing. It has been a real pleasure working with you all, thank you.

I also wish to thank my running mates for taking me away from the laptop and keeping me fit and active during a very intense ten weeks of writing – the fresh air and exercise have been invaluable! And of course, to all my family and friends for their wonderful love and encouragement – thank you!

Finally, a special mention to the children in my 'extended' family: Sophie and Amy, Emily, Tom, Luke and Beth, Amelia, Henry and the one on the way, and my two godsons, Mark and Tom. I hope one day you will read this book and discover for yourselves not only your incredible heritage, but also the amazing possibilities of the Christian life.

Endnotes

Introduction

[1] JHT speaking on 'Oh magnify the Lord with me!' quoted in M. Broomhall, *The Man Who Believed God (TMWBG)* (London: CIM, 1929) p202

[2] Taken from a letter from Hudson Taylor to William Berger dated 14 August 1870 and quoted in H. and G. Taylor's *Hudson Taylor and the China Inland Mission: The Growth of a Work of God (GOAWOG)* (London: China Inland Mission, 1911)

Chapter 1

[1] H. and G. Taylor, *Hudson Taylor in Early Years: The Growth of a Soul (GOAS)* (London: China Inland Mission, 1918) pp33–34

[2] The class leader was the spiritual leader of the people in a meeting. They kept track of attendance, visited people who missed the weekly meeting and provided support and encouragement as needed.

[3] Other connections included John Wesley, Dr Barnardo, George Muller, C.H. Spurgeon and Dwight Moody.

[4] H. and G. Taylor, *GOAS*, p22

[5] H. and G. Taylor, *GOAS*, p19

[6] H. and G. Taylor, *GOAS*, p25

[7] H. and G. Taylor, *GOAS*, p26

[8] Amelia and Benjamin are the author's great-grandparents; two of their sons were Noel and Marshall Broomhall. Marshall Broomhall was the author of *The Man Who Believed God* and many other related books. Noel Broomhall's son was Edwin James Broomhall, the author's father.

[9] M. Broomhall, *TMWBG*, pp14–15

[10] James Hudson Taylor (JHT), *A Retrospect* (London: China Inland Mission, 1951)

[11] All the references in this section are from M. Broomhall, *TMWBG*, Chapter Three.

[12] M. Broomhall, *Hudson Taylor's Legacy* (London: China Inland Mission, 1931) p48–49

[13] Irene Chang et al. *Christ Alone* (Hong Kong: OMF, 2005) p180

[14] M. Broomhall, *TMWBG*, p16

Chapter 2

[1] M. Broomhall, *TMWBG*, p20. JHT used to say this from four years old.

[2] M. Broomhall, *TMWBG*, p20–22. Peter Parley's book was originally published in 1843.

[3] M. Broomhall, *TMWBG*, p21

[4] John Bunyan, *Grace Abounding* (Oxford: Oxford University Press, 2008)

[5] M. Broomhall, *TMWBG*, p22

[6] JHT, *A Retrospect*, p11

[7] James Hudson Taylor wrote this in 1894 when he was 62 years of age, but does not mention a specific date. The actual date was sometime in June 1849, when Hudson was 17.

[8] JHT, *A Retrospect*, pp11–14

[9] JHT, *A Retrospect*, pp15–16

[10] JHT, quoted in M. Broomhall, *TMWBG*, p26

[11] JHT, quoted in H. and G. Taylor, *GOAS*, p78

[12] From a letter to his sister Amelia, Barnsley, 2 December 1849

[13] H. and G. Taylor, *GOAS*, p79

[14] Irene Chang et al., *Christ Alone*, p178

[15] JHT, quoted in Irene Chang et al., *Christ Alone*, p178

Chapter 3

[1] M. Broomhall, *TMWBG*, p29

[2] W.H. Medhurst, *China: Its State and Prospects, With Especial Reference to the Spread of the Gospel* (London: Forgotten Books, 2018)

[3] Hudson did this by comparing verses which contained the same words to create his own dictionary of Mandarin.

[4] From a letter to George Pearse in 1851

[5] Letter dated 21 April 1851 (for the full letter, see H. and G. Taylor, *GOAS*, pp101–104)

[6] M. Broomhall, *TMWBG*, p32

[7] JHT, *A Retrospect*, p17

[8] JHT, *A Retrospect*, p19

[9] H. and G. Taylor, *GOAS*, p95

[10] H. and G. Taylor, *GOAS*, p122

[11] H. and G. Taylor, *GOAS*, p123

[12] From a letter to his sister Amelia, 16 December 1851; the first part has not survived

[13] JHT, *A Retrospect*, pp20–21

[14] JHT, *A Retrospect*, pp23–24

[15] A.J. Broomhall, *Hudson Taylor and China's Open Century: Over the Treaty Wall (OTTW)* (Kent: Hodder and Stoughton, 1982) p51

[16] JHT, quoted in M. Broomhall, *TMWBG*, p43

[17] M. Broomhall reflected on JHT's 'faith abounding' in his book *Hudson Taylor's Legacy* (London: China Inland Mission, 1931) p48. The words are inspired by John Bunyan and his spiritual autobiography, *Grace Abounding*.

[18] JHT mentions in his autobiography, *A Retrospect* that this took place either the same evening as, or a few days after, the funeral of the Duke of Wellington, on 18 November 1852.

[19] JHT, *A Retrospect*, p32

[20] JHT, *A Retrospect*, p33

[21] JHT, *A Retrospect*, p38

[22] A.J. Broomhall, *OTTW*, p92

[23] H. and G. Taylor, *GOAS*, p126

[24] JHT, *A Retrospect*, Chapter 2

Chapter 4

[1] A.J. Broomhall, *OTTW*, p95. These were lines from a hymn composed (words and music) by Amelia Taylor and often sung by the family.

[2] For a more in-depth history and assessment of China at this time, see A.J. Broomhall, *Hudson Taylor and China's Open Century: Over the Treaty Wall* (Kent: Hodder and Stoughton, 1982). At this time, there were only 50 Protestant missionaries (not including wives) to the Chinese in East Asia, and the grand total of Chinese Protestant Christians was around 200, most of these in Malaysia.

[3] A.J. Broomhall, *OTTW*, p22

[4] M. Broomhall, *TMWBG*, p47

[5] A.J. Broomhall, *OTTW*, pp78–79

[6] A.J. Broomhall, *OTTW*, p81

[7] A.J. Broomhall, *OTTW*, p84

[8] A.J. Broomhall, *OTTW*, p124

[9] A.J. Broomhall, *OTTW* p124. Both enjoyed positions of responsibility and respect: Dr Medhurst was elected the first chairman of the Shanghai Municipal Society, and Dr Lockhurst ran a hospital situated on neutral ground.

[10] A.J. Broomhall, *OTTW*, p122

[11] A.J. Broomhall, *OTTW*, p120

[12] A.J. Broomhall, *OTTW*, p98

[13] Hudson Taylor, *A Retrospect*, p43

[14] From a booklet written by Amelia Taylor called *Parting Recollections*, quoted in H. and G. Taylor, *GOAS*, pp186–7

[15] JHT thought firstly that he would sail to China as assistant to the ship's surgeon. Failing that, as 'sailor before the mast', fully informing himself as to all that would be involved.

[16] JHT, *A Retrospect*, pp44–45

[17] JHT, *A Retrospect*, pp46–47

[18] *Amazing Grace*, John Newton

[19] Irene Chang et al., *Christ Alone*

[20] H. and G. Taylor, *GOAS*, p201

[21] H. and G. Taylor, *GOAS*, p203

[22] Irene Chang et al., *Christ Alone,* p180

[23] H. and G. Taylor, GOAWOG

Chapter 5

[1] H. and G. Taylor, *GOAS*, pp209–10

[2] H. and G. Taylor, *GOAS*, p226

[3] JHT, *A Retrospect*, p50

[4] A.J. Broomhall, *OTTW*, pp157–8

[5] H. and G. Taylor, *GOAS*, p254

[6] H. and G. Taylor, *GOAS*, p319

[7] JHT, *A Retrospect*, pp50–51

[8] From a reflection on Psalm 84 by C.H. Rappard-Gobat, director of the Pilgrim Mission of St Chrischona, near Basel, quoted in H. and G. Taylor, *GOAS*, p227. The Chrischona Mission supplied hundreds of missionaries to other societies, including the CIM.

[9] JHT, *A Retrospect*, pp71–72. Hudson Taylor devotes two chapters to the seven months he spent with William Burns, which perhaps indicates just how much importance he placed on this friendship.

[10] JHT, quoted in M. Broomhall, *TMWBG*, p75

[11] From a letter from JHT to his family in Barnsley, written six weeks after his wedding day

[12] JHT, *A Retrospect*, p75

[13] M. Broomhall, *TMWBG*, p91

[14] M. Broomhall, *TMWBG*, p93

[15] Written by JHT in Hangchow, China in 1868 in *China: Its Spiritual Need and Claims* (3rd ed.)

[16] From a reflection on Psalm 84 by C.H. Rappard-Gobat, director of the Pilgrim Mission of St Chrischona, near Basel, quoted in H. and G. Taylor, *GOAS*, p227

Chapter 6

[1] Hannah Hardey was a portrait painter, the artist of the oil painting of Hudson Taylor at the age of 21.

[2] The term 'China's Millions' was later to be used for the regular CIM publications designed to inform the world about the spiritual needs of China.

[3] M. Broomhall, *TMWBG*, p100

[4] JHT, quoted in M. Broomhall, *TMWBG*, p109

[5] M. Broomhall, *TMWBG*, p107

[6] This was due mainly to long hours and tiredness, and Rev Gough still grieving over the loss of his wife.

[7] For example, on Sunday 19 April 1863 he attended two services and walked to and from Tottenham, a total of 12 miles in total, while on 25 April he spent 13 and a half hours on the revision.

[8] H. and G. Taylor, *GOAWOG*, pp13–14

[9] When the house next door became available this was also rented by the Taylors to accommodate the increasing missionary household.

[10] JHT, *A Retrospect*, p112

[11] M. Broomhall, *TMWBG*, p106

[12] M. Broomhall, *TMWBG*, p101

[13] JHT, quoted in *GOAWOG*, p42

[14] JHT, quoted in *GOAWOG*, p42

[15] M. Broomhall, *TMWBG*, p109

[16] M. Broomhall, *TMWBG*, p171

[17] H. and G. Taylor, *GOAWOG*, pp444

[18] From an incomplete and undated letter to his mother, written sometime in 1854

Chapter 7

[1] JHT, *A Retrospect*, p111–112

[2] JHT, *A Retrospect*, p113–114

[3] M. Broomhall, *TMWBG*, p114

[4] JHT, quoted in M. Broomhall, *TMWBG*, p116

[5] Dr Martyn Lloyd-Jones, *Living Waters* (Illinois: Crossway Books, 2009) p328

[6] JHT, *A Retrospect*, p114

[7] M. Broomhall, *TMWBG*, p102. Later editions included maps, charts, diagrams and illustrations.

[8] M. Broomhall, *TMWBG*, p103

[9] JHT, quoted in M. Broomhall, *TMWBG*, p104

[10] JHT, *China's Spiritual Need and Claims (7th ed.)* (London: CIM, 1887) p48

[11] JHT, *China's Spiritual Need and Claims* p49

[12] A term used by Norman Cliff in his biography of Benjamin and Amelia Broomhall, *A Heart for China* (London: Authentic, 1998) p120

[13] Norman Cliff, *A Heart for China,* p45

[14] See Chapter 9.

[15] H. and G. Taylor, *GOAWOG*, p60

[16] H. and G. Taylor, *GOAWOG*, p183

[17] H. and G. Taylor, *GOAWOG*, p36

[18] A.J. Broomhall, *Hudson Taylor and China's Open Century, If I had A Thousand Lives* (Kent: Hodder & Stoughton, 1982) p442–443

[19] H. and G. Taylor, *GOAWOG*, p497

[20] H. and G. Taylor, *GOAWOG*, p418

Chapter 8

[1] From the poem, *The Voice of thy Brother's Blood*, by Henry Grattan Guinness quoted in H. and G. Taylor, *GOAWOG*, p70. Henry Grattan Guinness was the father of Geraldine Guinness who married Howard Taylor, JHT's son.

[2] M. Broomhall, *TMWBG*, p123–124

[3] The party consisted of Hudson and Maria Taylor, their four children (Gracie, Herbert, Frederick and Samuel), Lewis and Eliza Nicol, George Duncan, Josiah Jackson, William Rudland, John Sell, James Williamson, Susan Barnes, Mary Bausum, Emily Blatchley, Mary Bell, Mary Bowyer, Louise Degraz, Jane Faulding, Jane McClean and Elisabeth Rose.

[4] JHT quoted in M. Broomhall, *TMWBG*, p133

[5] M. Broomhall, *TMWBG*, p133

[6] For more information on this pioneering approach of Hudson Taylor, see Chapter 10 and the reflection 'Unity'.

[7] H. and G. Taylor, *GOAWOG*, p115

[8] All quotes in this section are taken from A.J. Broomhall, *Survivor's Pact* (London: Hodder & Stoughton, 1984) p359–365, unless otherwise stated.

[9] Gracie had become a Christian the year before. Hudson Taylor described the change that came over his young daughter at that time: 'Since her conversion she has become quite another child. Her look was more soft, more sweet, more happy.'

[10] From a reflection by John McCarthy, who was with the Taylors at the time

[11] M. Broomhall, *TMWBG*, p237

[12] From a letter to Amelia Broomhall dated 17 October 1869

[13] The 'Holiness' movement caused some controversy at the time, with some believing the tension between God's sovereignty and man's free-will to be out of balance. Language such as 'the second blessing' and 'sinless perfection' caused great concern. The influence of this movement on Hudson Taylor has led to criticism, but no evidence to suggest that Hudson Taylor's theology and practice was similarly out of balance. Roger Steer in his biography wrote: 'The Bergers, who were familiar with *The Revival* articles, expressed reservations about overstressing the passive, receptive aspect of holiness; they underlined the need for active resistance to evil and of effort to obey God. In his books a few years later, Bishop Ryle was also to correct what he considered to be the imbalance of the Keswick teaching. But there is no evidence that Hudson Taylor and his colleagues in China were deficient in effort or active service.' *J.Hudson Taylor, A Man In Christ* (Milton Keynes: Authentic Media, 1990) p238

[14] A letter from John McCarthy, in Hangzhou, to Hudson Taylor, received on 4 September 1869

[15] JHT in a letter dated 17 October 1869 quoted in full in H. and G. Taylor, *GOAWOG*, p173–177

[16] M. Broomhall, *TMWBG*, p130

[17] From a letter to William Berger, December 1869

[18] JHT, quoted in *GOAWOG*, p196–197

[19] JHT, quoted in M. Broomhall, *TMWBG*, p155

[20] From a little booklet called *Unfailing Springs* by JHT, published many years later. At the end he added some words of personal testimony, referring particularly to the events of 1870.

[21] From an article by JHT entitled *Blessed Adversity*

[22] H. and G. Taylor, *GOAWOG*, Chapter 14

[23] H. and G. Taylor, *GOAWOG*, Chapter 14

[24] H. and G. Taylor, *GOAWOG*, Chapter 14

[25] M. Broomhall, *TMWBG*, p4–5

[26] JHT in a letter to William Berger dated 14 August 1870

Chapter 9

[1] JHT, *Princely Service*, a Bible study on Numbers chapter 12, quoted in M. Broomhall, *TMWBG*, p167

[2] M. Broomhall, *TMWBG*, p165

[3] M. Broomhall, *TMWBG*, p169

[4] Mildmay Conference, Spring 1876

[5] JHT, quoted in M. Broomhall, *TMWBG*, p224

[6] JHT in a letter written in Salisbury, England to a fellow missionary in Yangzhou dated 8 February 1872

[7] JHT in a letter to a friend in China, written in April 1875 during his confinement for a spinal injury

[8] JHT in a letter to Amelia Taylor, a few weeks after landing in China in 1885

[9] JHT in a letter to Amelia Taylor written 9 November 1885

[10] JHT in a letter to Amelia Taylor written in January 1874 from a 'wretched inn' on a mountain road. Hudson was travelling across the snow-covered Chinese mountains to reach the sick child of a missionary couple.

[11] JHT, *Blessed Adversity*

[12] M. Broomhall, *TMWBG*, p133

[13] For more detailed accounts, see H. and G. Taylor, *GOAWOG*, pp216–433, and A.J. Broomhall, *China's Open Century* (vols. 5 and 6).

[14] Statistics taken from Irene Chang et al., *Christ Alone*, pp58,75

[15] Details taken from Irene Chang et al., *Christ Alone*, pp62–64

[16] H. and G. Taylor, *GOAWOG*, p378

[17] H. and G. Taylor, *GOAWOG*, p273

[18] H. and G. Taylor, *GOAWOG*, p299

[19] Judd, quoted in H. and G. Taylor, *GOAWOG*, pp328--9

[20] Irene Chang et al., *Christ Alone*, p70

[21] From the *History of the Church Missionary Society* (vol. 3) p285, quoted in *GOAWOG*, p384

[22] H. and G. Taylor, *GOAWOG*, p411

[23] Geraldine Taylor, *Pastor Hsi: Confucian Scholar and Conqueror of Demons* (London: CIM, 1900) foreword

[24] Jeanie Gray later married Herbert Taylor (eldest son of Hudson and Maria). They continued to serve in Yushan together.

[25] H. and G. Taylor, *GOAWOG*, p337

[26] H. and G. Taylor, *GOAWOG*, p252-253

[27] Dr Martyn Lloyd-Jones, *The Christian Warfare* (Edinburgh: The Banner of Truth Trust, 1976) p272

Chapter 10

[1] Words used by Hudson Taylor in a letter to his wife, Jennie, 6 July 1889, as he left for his second visit to America

[2] Places visited included: New York, Massachusetts, Chicago, St Louis, Niagara-on-the-Lake, Toronto, Vancouver and Montreal

[3] An eye-witness, quoted in *GOAWOG*, pp441–442

[4] JHT quoted in H. and G. Taylor, *GOAWOG*, p449

[5] H. and G. Taylor, *GOAWOG*, p457

[6] JHT, written on 11 January 1889, quoted in H. and G. Taylor, *GOAWOG*, p459

[7] H. and G. Taylor, *The Spiritual Secret of Hudson Taylor* (Pennsylvania: Whitaker House, 2003)

[8] H. and G. Taylor, *GOAWOG*, pp479–481

[9] JHT, quoted in *GOAWOG*, p482

[10] The formal name for a renewed strategy to evangelise the whole of China

[11] References in this section are taken from *GOAWOG*, Chapter 37

[12] At the end of March 1895, the mission numbered 621 members, settled in 122 central stations, 90 of which were in the 11 formerly unoccupied provinces.

[13] JHT in a letter home regarding his application to the Chinese Evangelisation Society, 18 June 1853

[14] Irene Chang et al., *Christ Alone*, pp174–175

Chapter 11

[1] Mari-Anna Auvinen-Pontinen and Jonas Adelin Jorgensen (eds.) *Mission and Money: Christian Mission in the Context of Global Inequalities* (Netherlands: Brill Academic Publishers, 2016) p154

[2] H. and G. Taylor, *GOAWOG*, p553

[3] All quotations in this section are taken from H. and G. Taylor, *GOAWOG*, chapters 39 and 40.

[4] H. and G. Taylor, *GOAWOG*, p595–596

[5] Dixon Hoste was married to Amelia Gertrude Broomhall, eldest child of Benjamin and Amelia Broomhall.

[6] H. and G. Taylor, *GOAWOG*, p614

[7] H. and G. Taylor, *GOAWOG*, p616–617

[8] See Chapter 1.

[9] Written by JHT in 1874 when he was in England and confined to bed. Quoted in Jim Cromarty, *It is not death to die* (Tain, Scotland: Christian Focus Publications, 2014)

[10] JHT in a letter to his sister, Amelia

[11] H. and G. Taylor, *GOAS*, pp141–142

[12] JHT in a letter to William Berger dated 14 August 1870, quoted in H. and G. Taylor, *GOAWOG*

[13] Conversion story of Confucian soldier in China in 1873 taken from *GOAWOG*, Chapter 16

Timeline: James Hudson Taylor

1749	Birth of James Taylor (great-grandfather)
1776	Marriage of James Taylor to Elizabeth Johnson
1778	Birth of John Taylor (grandfather)
1795	Death of James Taylor
1799	Marriage of John Taylor to Mary Shepherd
1807	Birth of James Taylor (father)
1808	Birth of Amelia Hudson (mother)
1831	Marriage of James and Amelia (parents)
1831	Consecration of firstborn to God
21 May 1832	Birth of James Hudson Taylor
1834	Death of John Taylor
1839	Methodist centenary celebrations
1846	Hudson Taylor's first spiritual experience
June 1849	Hudson Taylor's full conversion
Summer 1849	Call to service
December 1849	Call to China
1850	Death of Mary Taylor
May 1851	Moves to Hull
October 1852	Sails to London
November 1852	Starts work at the London Hospital
November 1852	Seriously infected and faces death
Winter 1852	Recovery and recuperation at home in Barnsley
January 1853	Returns to work in London
June 1853	Meets with Charles Bird (Chinese Evangelisation Society)
September 1853	Sails to China on board the *Dumfries*
1 March 1854	*Dumfries* embarks at Woosong; Hudson Taylor steps ashore on Chinese soil for the first time.

30 August 1854	Moved to house near North Gate
25 November 1854	Moved to house in London Missionary Society compound
Dec 1854 – Jan 1856	Ten inland evangelistic journeys
June 1855	Meets Maria Dyer for the first time in Ningbo
August 1855	Takes on Chinese dress
February 1856	Travels to Shanghai with William Burns
March 1856	Travels to Shantou
July 1856	Sails back to Shanghai; Burns and Taylor part
Oct 1856 – Jan 1857	Stationed in Ningbo
Jan – May 1857	Recalled to Shanghai; JHT resigns from CES; Amelia Taylor and Benjamin Broomhall engaged
May 1857	Returns to Ningbo
November 1857	Hudson and Maria engaged
20 January 1858	Hudson and Maria married
31 July 1859	Grace Hudson Taylor born
August 1859	Takes over hospital at Ningbo
June 1860	Closes hospital in Ningbo and moves back to Shanghai
July 1860	Taylors sail for home aboard the *Jubilee*
September 1860	CES disbanded
November 1860	Taylors arrive in England
April 1861	Birth of Herbert Hudson Taylor
July 1862	Hudson Taylor passes medical exams
October 1862	Hudson Taylor passes midwifery exams
November 1862	Birth of Frederick Howard Taylor
May 1864	Meets C.H. Spurgeon for the first time at the Metropolitan Tabernacle
June 1864	Birth of Samuel Dyer Taylor
September 1864	Taylor home moves to Coborn Street
June 1865	Vision on Brighton beach; first known use of the name 'China Inland Mission' (CIM)

October 1865	Publication of *China's Spiritual Need and Claims*; second property in Coborn Street rented
December 1865	Jane Dyer Taylor born and dies; first CIM day of fasting and prayer (New Year's Eve)
March 1866	First *Occasional Paper* printed
May 1866	Hudson Taylor, his family and a party of new missionaries sail for China on board the *Lammermuir*
25 October 1865	First edition of *China: Its Spiritual Need and Claims*
February 1866	Second edition
1 March 1866	First *Occasional Paper* (CIM 'magazine')
September 1866	*Lammermuir* arrives in Shanghai
Nov 1866 – Feb 1867	1 New Lane, Hangzhou rented; Maria Hudson Taylor (junior) born; Hudson Taylor sets up dispensary
May 1867	Hudson Taylor and Lewis Nicol sign the first CIM 'pact'
June 1867	Hudson Taylor goes on reconnaissance south-west of Hangzhou with McCarthy and Duncan
August 1867	Gracie Taylor dies
September 1867	Frederick Howard Taylor becomes a Christian
Nov – Dec 1867	Hudson Taylor and family travel to Huzhou
1868	Third edition of *China: Its Spiritual Need and Claims*
April 1868	Hudson Taylor and family journey up Grand Canal to Yangzhou
August 1868	Yangzhou riots; JHT and family forced to leave
September 1868	Completion of revision of Ningbo New Testament
November 1868	Hudson Taylor and family re-instated safely in Yangzhou; Charles Hudson Taylor born
September 1869	Hudson Taylor's 'personal Pentecost'
February 1870	Samuel Hudson Taylor dies (aged five)
March 1870	Emily Blatchley and Taylor children (except Charles) leave for England
July 1870	Noel Hudson Taylor born and dies; Maria Hudson Taylor dies; both buried in Zhenjiang Cemetery

August 1871	Hudson sails for England
November 1871	Hudson marries Jennie Faulding
March 1872	Resignation of William Berger as Home Director
August 1872	Home Council formed
October 1872	Hudson sails for China (third time) with Jennie Taylor
1872	Fourth edition of *China: Its Spiritual Need and Claims*
May 1874	Hudson falls and hurts spine
July 1874	Death of Emily Blatchley
October 1874	Hudson returns to England
January 1875	Appeal for the 'Eighteen'
July 1875	First publication of *China's Millions*
September 1876	Hudson sails for China (fourth time) without Jennie Taylor; Chefoo Convention signed
May 1877	General Missionary Conference, Shanghai
November 1877	Hudson sails for England
May 1878	Jennie Taylor sails for China without Hudson
August 1878	Hudson and Jennie Taylor holiday in Switzerland for the first time
February 1879	Hudson sails for China (fifth time)
Summer 1881	Death of Amelia Taylor (mother)
October 1881	Jennie Taylor sails for England
November 1881	Death of James Taylor (father); Hudson in Wuchang; appeal for the 'Seventy'
December 1881	Herbert Taylor arrives in China
February 1883	Hudson sails for England
1884	Fifth and sixth editions (name changed to *China's Spiritual Need and Claims*)
January 1885	Hudson sails for China (sixth time)
February 1885	'Cambridge Seven' sail for China
May–Oct 1886	Hudson travels to nine inland provinces

August 1886	Pastor Hsi ordained by Hudson Taylor
November 1886	First meeting of China Council; appeal for the 'Hundred'
1887	Seventh presentation edition of *China's Spiritual Need and Claims*
January 1887	Hudson sails for England
May 1887	Anniversary Meetings (21 years of CIM)
November 1887	Announcement of the 'Hundred' new workers and funds
December 1887	Sailing of the 'Hundred' to China
1887–1888	Henry Frost travels to London to meet Hudson Taylor
1888	Hudson arrives in North America with son Howard
1888	Hudson sails to China with American workers
1889	Hudson back in England; Auxiliary Council (Glasgow) formed; Ladies Council (London) formed; Hudson returns to North America; *To Every Creature* published; Hudson visits Sweden, Denmark and Norway
1890	Eighth edition of *China's Spiritual Need and Claims*; appeal for the 'Thousand' new CIM headquarters in Shanghai; Hudson sails for China (eighth time); Australian Council formed; first Australian worker to China; General Missionary Conference, Shanghai; German China Alliance formed; Hudson sails to Australia with M. Beauchamp; first Australasian party
1891	Sailing of first Scandinavian Party
1892	Hudson visits Vancouver and England
1893	Hudson visits Germany and Scotland
1894	Hudson sails for China (ninth time) via North America; Chino-Japanese War
1895	War ends; 1,153 new workers across 45 societies
1896	Hudson visits India; Hudson sails to England via Germany; Hudson visits Sweden, Norway and Germany; new CIM headquarters at Newington Green, London
1897	Hudson visits William Berger in France; Hudson visits Germany and Switzerland; Hudson Taylor's daughter, Maria, dies in China aged 30; Hudson sails for China (tenth time) via North America

1899   Hudson in Chongqing, Sichuan for West China Conference, Shanghai, Chefoo (Yantai), Mokanshan; Hudson leaves China for Australia and New Zealand with Jennie; close of work in China; Empress Dowager issues famous anti-foreign decree

1900   Hudson and Jennie Taylor and Dr and Mrs Howard Taylor visit New Zealand (January); New York Ecumenical Conference (April); Boxer Rebellion begins (May); Taylors reach England and proceed to Switzerland; Imperial decree ordering murder of all foreigners (June)

1901   Hudson falls in Chamounix Valley; Taylors visit England (winter)

Summer 1902   Hudson and Jennie Taylor in Chevalleyres, Switzerland

1903   Dixon Hoste formally appointed general director of CIM; Jennie Taylor ill with cancer; Hudson and Jennie Taylor in Lausanne (winter)

Spring 1904   Hudson and Jennie Taylor in Chevalleyres

July 1904   Death of Jennie Taylor

February 1905   Hudson travels to North America

17 April 1905   Hudson arrives in Shanghai (final visit to China)

3 June 1905   Death of Hudson Taylor in Chang-Sa, Hunan

J · HVDSON · TAYLOR ·

The Beloved Founder and Director of the China Inland Mission

BORN · 1832   DIED · 1905 ·

TAKE HOME THE
JAMES HUDSON TAYLOR DOCUDRAMA

Continue your discovery of James Hudson Taylor's story with the accompanying DVD docudrama. Filmed on location in the UK, Taiwan and China, this new production combines insightful narration from contemporary historians with dramatic re-enactments.

Suitable for you to enjoy by yourself, or together with your small group.

Produced by CTA/Gary Wilkinson. Running time: approx. 60 minutes EAN: 5027957-001701

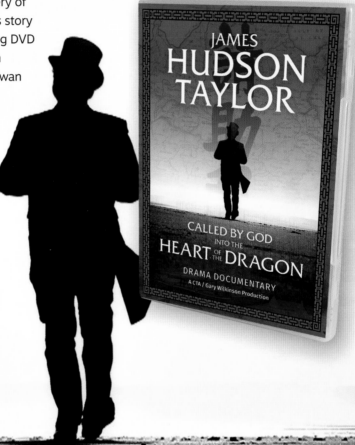

More biographies for you to enjoy...

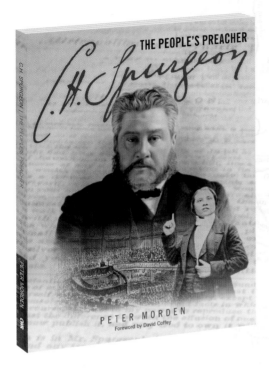

C.H. Spurgeon – The People's Preacher

Who was the man behind the headlines? Was he different in private to the way he appeared in public? What was his prayer life like and what was his attitude to the Bible? Did he have weaknesses and how were these overcome? All these questions are explored in this in-depth and inspiring biography by Peter Morden.

ISBN: 978-1-85345-497-4

John Bunyan – The People's Pilgrim

It may seem strange to us that someone could be held in prison for 12 years for refusing to stop preaching the gospel, but that's what happened to John Bunyan. Somehow, confined in his dirty, damp prison cell, Bunyan managed to pen *The Pilgrim's Progress*, one of the acknowledged classics of English literature. The book is an engaging and accessible account of this great man's life, with plenty of historical context and insight.

ISBN: 978-1-85345-836-1

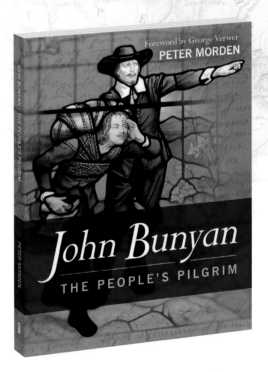

Transforming lives

CWR's vision is to enable people to experience personal transformation through applying God's Word to their lives and relationships.

Our Bible-based training and resources help people around the world to:
• Grow in their walk with God
• Understand and apply Scripture to their lives
• Resource themselves and their church
• Develop pastoral care and counselling skills
• Train for leadership
• Strengthen relationships, marriage and family life
  and much more.

Our insightful writers provide daily Bible reading notes and other resources for all ages, and our experienced course designers and presenters have gained an international reputation for excellence and effectiveness.

CWR's Training and Conference Centre in Surrey, England, provides excellent facilities in idyllic settings – ideal for both learning and spiritual refreshment.

CWR Applying God's Word
to everyday life and relationships

CWR, Waverley Abbey House,
Waverley Lane, Farnham,
Surrey GU9 8EP, UK

Telephone: +44 (0)1252 784700
Email: info@cwr.org.uk
Website: www.cwr.org.uk

Registered Charity No. 294387
Company Registration No. 1990308